Intermarriage
in the
United States

The *Marriage & Family Review* series:

Intermarriage
in the
United States

Gary A. Cretser and Joseph J. Leon
Co-Editors

Marriage & Family Review
Volume 5, Number 1

The Haworth Press
New York

The Haworth Press, Inc., 28 East 22 Street, New York, NY 10010

Library of Congress Cataloging in Publication Data
Main entry under title:

Intermarriage in the United States.

    (Marriage & family review ; v. 5, no. 1)
    Includes bibliographical references.
    1. Marriage, Mixed—United States—Addresses, essays, lectures.   2. Interracial marriage—United States—Addresses, essays, lectures.   3. Miscegenation—United States—Addresses, essays, lectures.   I. Cretser, Gary A.   II. Leon, Joseph J.
III. Series.
HQ536.I55   306.8'46'0973   82-6213
ISBN 0-917724-60-7   AACR2
ISBN 0-917724-83-6 (pbk.)

Intermarriage in the United States

Marriage & Family Review
Volume 5, Number 1

CONTENTS

EDITOR'S INTRODUCTION

Interfaith and interracial marriage is not a "hot" topic for research. The subject attracts a few discerning and inquiring thinkers whose ideas extend beyond the boundaries of ethnicity. Marriages across racial and cultural boundaries have been studied usually from a problems stance. The research orientation is toward discerning difficulties and failures and to ignore the positives and successes of such arrangements.

This special volume is refreshing in its treatment of interracial and intercultural marriage. The authors are objective in their reports, human in expressing their views, and thorough in their coverage of available data. They provide adequate explanations and leave the reader with sufficient alternative views to experience learning, confirmation, or change in one's position on inter-ethnic marriage. Gary Cretser and Joseph Leon are to be congratulated for their excellent work as special issue co-editors. This volume will be read and referenced by students and scholars for years to come.

Marvin B. Sussman
Editor
Marriage & Family Review

INTERMARRIAGE IN THE U.S.:
AN OVERVIEW OF THEORY AND RESEARCH

Gary A. Cretser
Joseph J. Leon

Since the early 1900s American sociologists and other social scientists have periodically engaged in the study of intermarriage. The belief has been that this type of study may provide answers to a whole host of questions about social life within and between racial, religious, and national origin groups in American society (Barron, 1951). Only in a relatively few instances have these studies attempted to link the data to a particular theory. More often than not the theories and findings have not been cumulative. Nevertheless some attempts (i.e., Barnett, 1963; Barron, 1951) have been made to sort out the research. In this paper, a summary of theoretical and methodological contributions to the intermarriage literature is attempted.

It must be remembered that as late as 1966 seventeen states had formal prohibitions against one or more forms of interracial marriage. The United States Supreme Court overturned the sixteen existing state anti-miscegenation statutes with a decision rendered June 12, 1967. At one time or another, forty of the fifty states have had laws which prohibited blacks from intermarrying with whites. Pennsylvania, in 1780, was the first state to repeal its anti-miscegenation law, while Indiana and Wyoming took this action as recently as 1965.

As Weinberger (1966:158) has pointed out, the various statutes were not uniform. For example, in Arkansas a person "who has in her or his veins any negro blood whatever" was forbidden from marrying a white person. More commonly the laws specified that only persons with one-eighth or more such blood or those related within three generations to a member of a particular racial group were so prohibited. Aside from regular prohibitions against marriages of blacks and whites, other groups mentioned in one or more statutes included West Indians, Japanese, Chinese, Mongolians, Indians, and Malayans. An example is California, where whites were prohibited from marrying Mongolians beginning in 1905 and Malayans beginning in 1933. Both of these statutes were held unconstitutional in the Perey vs. Zippold case of 1948 (Cretser, 1967).

Gary A. Cretser, PhD, and Joseph J. Leon, PhD, are affiliated with the Behavioral Science Department, California State Polytechnic University, Pomona. An earlier version of this paper was presented at the Annual Pacific Sociological Association Meetings in Anaheim, CA, April 1979.

3

Theoretical Contributions

A number of theoretical perspectives have been presented to explain intermarriage. These perspectives vary by the type of intermarriage considered. The assimilation perspective has been and continues to be, used widely to account for interethnic and interreligious marriage. Hypergamy has been used primarily to explain marriage defined as interracial. Also, at the psychological level, oedipal and rebellion-rejection models continue to be used to interpret interracial intermarriage. Additionally, a demographic orientation has been taken in arriving at explanations for marriage between ethnic, racial and religious groups. In this section each of these perspectives is summarized.

Assimilation

Bossard noted in 1939 that the sociological study of intermarriage, especially between different nationalities, had been neglected. He suggested that the study of intermarriage was important because it indexed the assimilation process and degree of social distance, as well as aiding in understanding family life and personality problems.

Kennedy (1944) associated intermarriage with assimilation among white ethnics in New Haven. She suggested that intermarriage can be thought of both as an indicator of the degree of assimilation occurring in the society and as a means of promoting assimilation itself. Kennedy found that at least among white ethnics, intermarriage was increasingly common but largely occurred within major religious groupings (i.e., triple melting pot). On the other hand, Bugelski (1961) found that the 1960 residents of Buffalo with Polish or Italian names, when compared to the 1930 residents, were intramarrying at a declining rate. In fact he expected such marriages to become rare by 1975, but added that he was not able to draw any strong conclusions from his preliminary investigation. Marcson (1950) also takes issue with the notion that intermarriage can be thought of as an index of assimilation and instead argues that this assumption is fallacious. He points out if intermarriage was functionally interrelated with assimilation, intermarriage ratios would be higher for the oldest ethnic groups and lowest for those most recently arrived. Marcson (1950:77) suggests that conditions which facilitate intermarriage are "high education, middle class status, middle income, professional and proprietory occupations, second and third generations, and rural nonfarm residence." His position is actually very similar to that of Kennedy in that he expects intermarriage between ethnic groups to occur much more often than between individuals representing differing religious groups or social classes.

Price and Zubrzycki (1962), in an article primarily concerned with the proper techniques of constructing assimilation indices, take issue with Marcson's assumptions. They point out that Marcson does not recognize the distinction between the process of integration and that of assimilation. Further, they point out that by definition integration is only one element of the broader process of assimilation, whereas assimilation in its fullest sense also includes physical amalgamation through inter-marriage, economic absorption and social acculturation.

An assimilation approach to understanding intermarriage is also taken by Parkman and Sawyer (1967) in dealing with this phenomenon in Hawaii. They developed a combined index to measure the variation in race, religion, and nationality for mar-riages. From their data analysis, two dimensions of intermarriage were observed. One, they labeled East-West (a measure of the extent to which a group has acquired the dominant contemporary way of life) and; two, urbanicity (percentage of the group living in Honolulu). According to this model, intermarriage rates will be highest be-tween groups who are similar on these two dimensions.

A broader model of assimilation developed by Milton M. Gordon (1964) uses intermarriage as a definition of marital assimilation. He views marital assimilation as an "inevitable by-product of structural assimilation" (Gordon, 1964:80). Accord-ing to Gordon, it is one of the seven types of assimilation necessary before full assimilation into a host society can occur.

Hypergamy

In addition to the various assimilation approaches, hypergamy has been another major theoretical thread in the study of intermarriage. Davis (1941) was one of the first theorists to suggest that interracial marriage can be understood in terms of its function for the upper caste or class. He argues that an upper caste or subcaste male exchanges his social position for the achievement, beauty, intelligence, youth, or wealth brought to the marriage by the female partner of a lower caste or subcaste. Davis hypothesized that when intermarriage does occur it is likely to be hypergamous, i.e., the female marrying upward in terms of caste position. However, in dealing with black and white intermarriage in the United States, by far the most common form involves a black male and a white female. To explain this phenomena Davis suggests that in the United States we have a philosophy embracing equalitarian democracy rather than a caste system. This enables black males who have higher socioeconomic status to exchange this resource for the higher ethnic status of the white females who stand low socioeconomically. This process is one of class hypergamy rather than caste hypergamy.

Merton (1941:372) has added support to the theoretical position that black-white intermarriage can be expected to conform to a class hypergamous pattern. Merton would expect marriages involving a lower class white woman and an upper class black man to occur most frequently "for it involves a reciprocal compensatory situa-tion in which the negro male exchanges his higher economic position for the white female's higher caste position." Van Den Berghe (1960) modified the hypergamy argument suggesting that the principle at work is maximization of status. Intermar-riage of a hypergamous nature would occur when the female can obtain a status gain for herself or her children and the male would suffer no substantial loss of status for himself.

Monahan (1976), in a study of interracial marriages, found that a white spouse in a black/white marriage was more often in a higher occupational status when compared to white/white marriages. This is contrary to the relationship suggested by Davis (1941) and Merton (1941). In addition, Heer (1974:246), using 1960 and 1970 census data, found no support for the class hypergamy position when education is the measure "unless the availability of marriage partners by educational attainment is held constant."

Psychological/Psychoanalytic

Several writers have dealt with intermarriage in terms of the psychological conditions manifested by the marriage partners rather than existing social conditions. The behavior of intermarrying can be viewed through this approach as the acting out of a variety of psychological problems. Freeman (1955:377) has suggested the following propositions to account for certain individuals intermarrying:

> (1) Individuals who intermarry feel they have been rejected by their own groups. (2) They become hostile or rebellious toward their own groups and their symbols. (3) They are exposed to a new and rejected group. (4) They identify with this new group, internalize its norms, and idealize its way of life. (5) Dating and mate selection follow identification with this new group. (6) Only rebels from the new group can be attracted, so that the pairs will possess similar psychological backgrounds and patterns of social adjustment. (7) The social distance between the individual's own group and the group in which he selects a mate will be a positive function of the amount of his hostility toward his own group.

Resnik (1933), in dealing primarily with religious intermarriage, suggests that persons who intermarry are one of four types: "(1) The emancipated person. (2) The rebellious person. (3) The detached person. (4) The adventurous person." He further points out that certain of the wishes suggested by W. I. Thomas can be obtained through intermarrying. Grier and Cobbs (1968) and more recently Kelley (1976), have discussed in some detail what they consider to be the subconscious motivation associated with black and white sexual relations. This explanation involves the inadequate repression of attraction to the opposite sex parent. This attraction leads the individual to select a spouse who is different from that parent, vis., racially. Grier and Cobbs (1968) have suggested that for the black male and white female each can provide the other with the opportunity to manage their oedipal/incest fantasies. In addition, beliefs of sexual and sensual superiority and the opportunity to act out racial hostility through sexual behavior combine to make this interracial combination more likely to occur. Also in the psychoanalytic realm of explanation, Biegel (1966) and Brayboy (1966) propose respectively, that self-esteem and guilt theories apply to understanding the motivation for interracial marriage. Individuals with low self-esteem and/or feelings of inferiority may marry a member of a lower status group because they view themselves as deserving no better. The member of the lower status group intermarries in an overcompensation process. Guilt associated with a need to punish oneself may also be linked to intermarriage especially between black and white individuals. Brayboy argues that such intermarriage is necessarily associated with the history of black exploitation by whites in this country.

Very little systematic effort has been made to develop these various theoretical fragments into a testable framework. For the most part they are highly speculative, involve concepts inadequately defined, and were generated from case studies. Porterfield (1978:84), in reviewing the various explanations suggested above, found they had little explanatory value in terms of his sample of black/white marriages. In fact, he concludes with the statement "this group's motives for marriage do not appear to be any different from those individuals marrying in the conventional style."

Sex Ratio and Group Size

Although there have been relatively few theoretical approaches suggested in the literature as explanatory frameworks for intermarriage, early research by Bogardus (1937), Catapusan (1938), and Panunzio (1942) suggested that intermarriage could be related to an unbalanced sex ratio. This approach was primarily associated with accounting for the high rate of intermarriage among Filipino males who greatly outnumbered the supply of available Filipino females. Barron (1946) also pointed out that an unbalanced sex ratio combined with relatively small numerical representation is associated with higher rates of intermarriage between certain groups. Barron (1946:262) further suggests that "the sex ratio of one group, however, is ineffective in inducing either intra or intermarriage unless it is complemented by the same or other factors in other groups." Burma (1963) suggested this as a factor useful in explaining intermarriage in Los Angeles while Yamamoto (1973:317) and Parkman and Sawyer (1967) indicate that an unbalanced sex ratio appears to be responsible for intermarriage initially in Hawaii at least among some racial groups. Today the Department of Health in Hawaii collects marriage data by bride and groom so that sex ratio, at least for the marriage population, can be taken into account.

Propinquity

Propinquity, according to Barron (1946:275), is "of tremendous importance in partially determining intermarriage incidence and selection." He argues that other social and demographic factors are ineffective without propinquity and similarity of culture.

Golden (1959) found that propinquity was a factor in explaining mate selection for his intermarried sample. Propinquity in terms of employment, commercial transactions, education, recreation, and voluntary organizations were all cited as being associated with interethnic marriage. Heer (1966) determined that residential segregation was related to variations in black/white intermarriage proportions. Metropolitan areas in California which had high coefficients of dissimilarity tended to have low ratios of actual to expected intermarriage. Heer (1966) further found that large status differences between blacks and whites within California S.M.S.A.'s and for the states of Michigan and Nebraska were associated with lower actual to expected ratios of black/white marriage. Heer concludes that the increasing actual to expected ratios of black/white marriage in general may be explained by: (1) decreasing residential segregation, (2) decreasing variation between black and white socio-economic status, and (3) increasing societal tolerance for this type of intermarriage.

Computational Methods Used in the Reporting of Intermarriage

In the past five decades a number of computational methods have been used in an effort to standardize and summarize the extent of intermarriage. In this section a listing and summary of these methods are presented.

The rate or percent intermarriage is a formulation which is frequently used. However, there is often confusion as to whether the percent intermarriage reported is for individuals or for marriages. Both Besanceney (1965) and Rodman (1965) agree that these rates need to be distinguished.

The difference between these two formulations is that on the one hand, the group is counted once (marriages) and on the other, each marriage is counted twice (i.e., one for each partner; individual). The effect is that the extent of intermarriage appears less when an individual rate if intermarriage is used. (See example below.)

Hypothetical Data

	Black Females	White Females	Total
Black Males	20	10	30
White Males	5	35	40
Total	25	45	70

Percent black mixed marriage for *individual's* marrying is:

$$\frac{\text{total blacks intermarrying}}{\text{total blacks marrying}} \times 100 = \frac{15}{55} \times 100 = 27.3\%$$

Percent black mixed marriage for *marriages* is:

$$\frac{\text{total blacks intermarrying}}{\text{total blacks marrying}} \times 100 = \frac{15}{35} \times 100 = 42.9\%$$

Rodman (1965) suggested that once you know the percent of one type of marriage rate you can find the percent for the other type. Formulas for the conversions are as follows:

For mixed marriage percent for marriages (x): $x = 200y/100 + y$. For mixed marriage percent for individuals (y): $y = 100x/200 - x$.

Besanceney (1965) and Glick (1970) suggest that group size affects the extent of intermarriage and should be acknowledged as operating through mathematical necessity. (For rationale see Sex Ratio and Group Size Section). To accomplish this a ratio of actual to expected rates is constructed. The formula is: $R = 1 - Fe/Fo$, where: Ratio of Actual to expected = R; Observed rate = Fo; Expected = Fe. Besanceney (1965) suggests that when possible this ratio be reported. This procedure has caught on to some degree in the study of intermarriage.

A similar approach has been used by Barnett (1963) and Aldridge (1973). This approach employs the x^2 statistic and attempts to answer the question, is the rate of intermarriage significantly different between time periods.

Another technique different in intent is used to describe, in summary manner, the proportion of mixed marriages of a particular group by comparing it to all mixed marriages. The denominator is all mixed marriages and the extent of intermarriage for the group is expressed as a percent (Glick, 1970) or rate (Burma, 1952) where all mixed marriages equal 100% or 100. Example for percent:

$$\frac{\text{no. intermarriages for group}}{\text{no. of intermarriages for all groups}} \times 100 = X\%$$

Indices in the past 15 years have been developed to show the extent of intermarriage but have not been widely used. Burma (1963:160) employed an index that controls for the size of each group in the population. Example: Index = PI/PTP. Where the index value is equal to the percent intermarried (PI) divided by percent of individuals of that ethnic group in the total population (PTP). The resulting statistic will vary from 0 to 100. The higher values indicate a greater proportion of intermarriage. The statistic has value when several ethnic groups are being compared.

Two other techniques use extent of intermarriage as a variable to show intermarriage distance or marriage distance. These techniques standardize and compare groups with each other. Parkman and Sawyer (1967:598) developed and used the construct "intermarriage distance," where the greater the distance the less the intermarriage. Example:

$$\text{Intermarriage Distance} = \text{Log} \frac{(\text{Within A}) (\text{Within B})}{(1/2 \text{ Between})}$$

A technique somewhat similar to Heer (1966), cited previously, was used by Leon (1975). This technique produces an index termed "marriage distance" which indicates the extent to which the observed marriages of each possible combination of marriages deviate in percentage and direction from the expected marriages for each possible combination of marriages.

$$\text{Marriage Distance} = \frac{Fo - Fe}{Fe} \times 100$$

Taken together the computational techniques presented suggest quite different answers to the question what is the extent of intermarriage. In the next sections the correlates of interethnic marriage and social attitudes toward intermarriage are summarized.

Correlates

In addition to the findings on rates of intermarriage, a number of characteristics have been associated with intermarrying individuals and couples in the research literature. Risdon (1954) found that interracially marrying males in Los Angeles were older on the average than a control group of intraracially marrying males. However, interracially marrying females were younger than their control group. Data analyzed by Burma (1963) and Cretser (1967) for Los Angeles County demonstrated that intermarrying brides and grooms were significantly (statistical) older than intramarrying individuals.

Pavela (1964) supports this association with data on a small Indiana sample. Additionally, findings for Indiana generated by Monahan (1973) suggest that in black and white marriages, spouses, except for black females, were older on the average than the spouses in comparable intramarriages. Looking at mixed marriages in general, Monahan concludes that age tends to have an intermediate position between the two age patterns of the races involved. However, Schmitt and Souza (1963) found that in Hawaii male and female partners in interracial households were younger than intraracial spouses.

Burma (1963) found that intermarriages involving blacks were most likely to include previously divorced persons. However, most other intermarriages which he investigated were less likely to involve divorced persons than white/white marriages. Cretser (1967) found that both intermarrying brides and intermarrying grooms when compared with intramarrying brides and grooms were significantly more likely to have been married previously. These findings are similar to those of Pavela (1964) who found that in his sample of black/white marriages, black brides and grooms were more likely to have been married previously when compared to their white spouses. Monahan (1973) also found that intermarriages generally involved fewer "primary marriages" (a first marriage for both the bride and groom).

Bean and Aiken (1976) investigated fertility as it relates to religious intermarriage and found that a higher rate of unwanted fertility is associated with these marriages than with intrareligious marriages. Heer (1974) reports that for the U.S. as a whole, the average number of children born to interracial couples is less than to homogeneous black couples and similar to the norm for white/white marriages.

There is conflicting evidence with regard to the rate of divorce for intermarrying vs. intramarrying couples. Lynn (1953) found that black/white marriages in Washington, D.C. had a failure rate approximately equal to that of intraracial couples. Cheng and Yamamura (1957) report that for Hawaii the divorce rate for outmarriages was substantially higher than for inmarriages.

Monahan (1970) reports that data from Iowa indicates that black/white marriages are more stable than black/black marriages and that black husbands with white wives have a lower divorce rate than white couples. Heer (1974) argues that in comparing black/white couples with white/white and black/black couples married in 1950–60 and still married in 1970, a significant difference in stability exists. Intermarried couples were substantially less likely to still be married than either of the intramarried groups.

Social Attitudes

With increasing intermarriage, there has been a change in societal attitudes. Heer (1966), in pointing out the increased ratios of actual to expected intermarriage in several states, suggests that increasing tolerance may account for it. To substantiate this position he cited statistics showing the sharp increase in the percentage of white students favoring black and white students in the same schools over the period 1942 to 1963.

An article more directly related to this hypothesis (Leon, 1977) compared the responses from the NORC General Social Survey over the period 1972, 1973, and 1974. To the questions, "Do you think there should be laws against marriages between Negroes and Whites?"; 38% of the white respondents answered "yes" in 1972, 37% "yes" in 1973, and 34% "yes" in 1974, and 38% in 1975 which indicated a rather consistent degree of tolerance of black/white marriages.

General Findings

Interracial (black) and interethnic (Spanish surnamed) marriages account for 3% of all marriages in the U.S. today. In 1977 there were 421,000 interracial marriages, 2.4 million Spanish origin mixed marriages out of a total of 48 million marriages. (U.S. Bureau of the Census, 1978). However, there has been little recent (during the last 15 years) research on white ethnics intermarrying with each other, while there has been continued interest and research on non-white ethnic intermarriage.

Findings indicate that intermarriage is increasing for all categories but ethnic intramarriage remains the statistical norm for the American population. If there is a change in the rate of intermarriage it will probably increase due primarily to the societal movement toward equal status and increased social acceptance of intermarriage.

In the articles which follow each author(s) examines the data on intermarriage involving a specific ethnic group or in the case of Hawaii several ethnic groups. In every article an attempt has been made to review and synthesize significant contributions.

REFERENCES

Adams, R. *Interracial Marriage in Hawaii*. New York: Macmillan, 1937.

Aldridge, Delores A. "The Changing Nature of Interracial Marriage in Georgia: A Research Note." *Journal of Marriage and the Family*, 1973, *35*: 641–642.

Alvirez, David and Frank D. Bean. "The Mexican American Family." In C. Mindel and R.W. Habenstein (eds.), *Ethnic Families in America*. New York: Elsevier, 1976.

Barber, K.E. "An Analysis of Intrafaith and Interfaith Marriage in Indiana," Ph.D. dissertation, Purdue University; Ann Arbor, Michigan: University Microfilms, 1967.

Barlow, Brent A. "Notes on Mormon Interfaith Marriages." *The Family Coordinator*, 1977, 26: 143-150.

Barnett, Larry D. "Interracial Marriage in California." *Marriage and Family Living*, 1963, (Nov.): 424-427.

Barnett, Larry D. "Research on International and Interracial Marriages." *Marriage and Family Living*, 1963, 25: 105-107. (a)

Barron, Milton L. *People Who Intermarry*. Syracuse, N.Y., Syracuse University Press, 1946.

Barron, Milton L. "Research on Intermarriage: A Survey of Accomplishments and Prospects." *American Journal of Sociology*, 1951, 57: 251.

Bean, Frank D. and Benjamin S. Bradshaw. "Intermarriage Between Persons of Spanish and Non-Spanish Surname: Changes From the Mid-Nineteenth to the Mid-Twentieth Century." *Social Science Quarterly*, 1976, 51: 389-395.

Bean, Frank D. and Linda H. Aiken. "Intermarriage and Unwanted Fertility in the United States." *Journal of Marriage and the Family*, 1976, 38: 61-67.

Besanceney, Paul H. "On Reporting Rates of Intermarriage." *American Journal of Sociology*, 1965, 70: 717-721.

Biegel, H.G. "Problems and Motives in Interracial Relationships." *The Journal of Sex Research*, 1966, 2: 185-205.

Bogardus, E.S. "Filipino Americans." In F.S. Brown and J.S. Roucek, *Our Racial Minorities*. New York: Prentice-Hall, Inc., 1937.

Bossard, James H.S. "Nationality and Nativity as Factors in Marriage." *American Sociological Review*, 1939, 4: 792-798.

Bradshaw, Benjamin S. "Some Demographic Aspects of Marriage: A Comparative Study of Three Ethnic Groups." Master's thesis, University of Texas, 1960.

Brayboy, Thomas L. "Interracial Sexuality as an Expression of Neurotic Conflict." *Journal of Sex Research*, 1966, 2: 3, 179-184.

Bugelski, B.R. "Assimilation Through Intermarriage." *Social Forces*, 1961, 40: 148-153.

Bumpass, Larry. "The Trends of Interfaith Marriage in the United States." *Social Biology*, 1970, 17: 253-259.

Burchinal, Lee G. and Loren E. Chancellor. "Proportions of Catholics, Urbanism, and Mixed-Catholic Marriage Rates Among Iowa Counties." *Social Problems"*, 1963.

Burma, John H. "Research Note on the Measurement of Interracial Marriage." *American Journal of Sociology*, 1952, 57: 587-589.

Burma, John H. "Interethnic Marriage in Los Angeles, 1948-1959." *Social Forces*, 1963, 42: 156-165.

Burma, John H., Gary A. Cretser, and Joseph J. Leon. "Confidential and Non-Confidential Marriage: A Study of Spanish-Surnamed Marriage in San Bernardino County, California, 1970-1977." Paper presented at the annual meeting of the Western Social Science Association, Denver, Colorado, April, 1978.

Catapusan, Benicio T. "Filipino Intermarriage Problems in the United States." *Sociology and Social Research*, 1938, 22: 265-272.

Chancellor, Loren E. and Thomas P. Monahan. "Religious Preference and Interreligious Mixtures in Marriages and Divorces in Iowa." *American Journal of Sociology*, 1955, 61: 233-239.

Cheng, C.K. and D.S. Yamamura. "Interracial Marriage and Divorce in Hawaii." *Social Forces*, 1957, 36: 77-84.

Cretser, Gary A. "An Investigation of Interethnic Marriage in Los Angeles County 1950-1961: and Its Relation to Selected Demographic Factors." Unpublished M.A. Thesis, University of Southern California, 1967.

Davis, James. A. "Codebook for Spring 1975 General Social Survey." National Opinion

Research Center, University of Chicago, Distributed by Roper Public Opinion Research Center: Williamston, MA, 1975.

Davis, Kingsley. "Intermarriage in Caste Societies." *American Anthropologist*, 1941, *43*(3), 376–395.

Farber, Bernard, Leonard Gordon, and Albert J. Mayer. "Intermarriage and Jewish Identity." Paper presented at the annual meetings of American Sociological Association, San Francisco, 1978.

Freeman, Linton. "Homogamy in Interethnic Mate Selection." *Sociology and Social Research*, *39*: 369–377.

Glick, Paul C. "Intermarriage Among Ethnic Groups in the United States." *Social Biology*, 1970, *17*: 292–298.

Goldberg, Nathan. "Jewish Population in the U.S." *The Jewish People Past and Present*, Vol. II, Jewish Encyclopedia Handbook, 1948.

Golden, Joseph. "Facilitating Factors in Negro-White Intermarriage." *Phylon*, 1959, *20*: 273–284.

Gonzalez, Nancie L. "The Spanish Americans of New Mexico: A Distinctive Heritage." Advance Report 9, Mexican American Study Project, Los Angeles: University of California at Los Angeles Graduate School of Business Administration, 1967.

Gordon, Milton. *Assimilation in American Life*. New York: Oxford University Press, 1964.

Grier, William H. & Price M. Cobbs. *Black Rage*. New York: Basic Books, 1968.

Heer, David M. "Negro-White Marriage in the United States." *Journal of Marriage and the Family*, August 1966, 262–273.

Heer, David M. "The Prevalence of Black-White Marriage in the United States, 1960 and 1970." *Journal of Marriage and the Family*, 1974, *36*: 246–258.

Heiss, Jerold S. "Premarital Characteristics of the Religiously Intermarried in an Urban Area." *American Sociological Review*, 1960, *25*: 47–55.

Kelley, Michael. "Some Psychological and Sociological Factors Influencing Motivation for Interracial Marriage." Ph.D. dissertation, California School of Professional Psychology, Los Angeles, 1976.

Kennedy, Ruby Jo Reeves. "Premarital Residential Propinquity and Ethnic Endogamy." *American Journal of Sociology*, 1943, *48*: 5, 580–584.

Kennedy, Ruby Jo Reeves. "Single or Triple Melting Pot? Intermarriage Trends in New Haven, 1870–1940." *American Journal of Sociology*, 1944, *49*: 331–339.

Kimura, Akeim and Harry H.L. Kitano. "Interracial Marriage: A Picture of the Japanese Americans." *Journal of Social Issues*, 1974, *29*: 2, 67–81.

Leon, Joseph J. "Sex-Ethnic Marriage in Hawaii: A Nonmetric Multi-dimensional Analysis." *Journal of Marriage and the Family*, Nov. 1975, 775–781.

Leon, Joseph J. "White Attitudes Towards Antimiscegenation Law 1974: A Hypotheses Test and Analysis of Selected Socio-Demographic Variables." *The Marriage and Family Counselors Quarterly*, 1977, *2*: 47–56.

Lynn, A.Q. "Interracial Marriage in Washington, D.C. 1940–1947." Ph.D. dissertation, Catholic University of America (unpublished), 1953.

Marcson, Simon. "A Theory of Intermarriage and Assimilation." *Social Forces*, 1950, *29*: 75–78.

Massarik, Fred. "The Jewish Population of San Francisco, Marin County and the Peninsula, 1959." San Francisco: The Jewish Welfare Federation, 1959.

Merton, Robert K. "Intermarriage and Social Structure: Fact and Theory." *Psychiatry*, 1941, *4*: 361–374.

Mittelbach, Frank G., Joan W. Moore and Ronald McDaniel. "Intermarriage of Mexican Americans." Advance Report 6, Mexican American Study Project Los Angeles: University of California Graduate School of Business Administration, 1966.

Monahan, Thomas P. "Are Interracial Marriages Really Less Stable?" *Social Forces*, 1970, *48*: 461–473.

Monahan, Thomas P. "Some Dimensions of Interreligious Marriages in Indiana, 1962–1967."

Social Forces, 1973, *52*: 195–203.

Monahan, Thomas P. "Marriage Across Racial Lines in Indiana." *Journal of Marriage and the Family*, 1973, *35*: 632–640. (a)

Monahan, Thomas P. "An Overview of Statistics on Interracial Marriage in the United States with Data on Its Extend From 1963–1970." *Journal of Marriage and the Family*, May 1976, 223–231.

Monahan, Thomas P. "The Occupational Class of Couples Entering Into Interracial Marriages." *Journal of Comparative Family Studies*, 1976, *7*, 2: P175–192. (a)

Murgia, Edward and L. Parker Frisbie. "Trends in Mexican American Intermarriage: Recent Findings in Perspective." *Social Science Quarterly*, 1977, *58*: 374–389.

Nelson, Bryce. "Marriages Between Black, Whites Up 36% Since 1970." *Los Angeles Times*: Jan. 14th, 1979.

Omatsu, G. "Nichonmachi Beat." *Hokubei Mainichi*: Jan. 12, 1972.

Panunzio, Constantine. "Intermarriage in Los Angeles, 1924–1933." *American Journal of Sociology*, 1942, *47*: 690–701.

Parkman, Margaret A. and Jack Sawyer. "Dimensions of Ethnic Intermarriage in Hawaii." *American Sociological Review*, 1967, *32*: 4, 593–608.

Pavela, Todd H. "An Exploratory Study of Negro-White Intermarriage in Indiana." *Journal of Marriage and the Family*, 1964, *26*:209–211.

Porterfield, Ernest. *Black and White Mixed Marriages*. Chicago: Nelson-Hall, 1978.

Price, C.A. and J. Zubrzycki. "The Use of Inter-Marriage Statistics as an Index of Assimilation." *Population Studies*, 1962, *16*: 58–69.

Resnik, Reuben B. "Some Sociological Aspects of Intermarriage of Jew and Non-Jew." *Social Forces*, 1933, *11*: 94–102.

Risdon, R. "A Study of Interracial Marriages Based on Data for Los Angeles County." *Sociology and Social Research*, 1954, *39*: 92–95.

Rodman, Hyman. "Technical Note on Two Rates of Mixed Marriage." *American Sociological Review*, 1965, *30*: 776–778.

Rosenthal, Erich. "Some Recent Studies About the Extent of Jewish Out-Marriage in the U.S.A." *Intermarriage and Jewish Life*. New York: The Herzl Press and the Jewish Reconstructionalist Press, 1963.

Rosenthal, Erich. "Jewish Intermarriage in Indiana." *Eugenics Quarterly*, 1968, *15*: 277–287.

Schmitt, Robert C. and Robert A. Souza. "Social & Economic Characteristics of Interracial Households in Honolulu." *Social Problems*, Winter 1963, X, No. 3, pp. 264–68.

Schwartz, Shepard. "Mate Selection Among New York City's Chinese Males 1931–38." *American Journal of Sociology*, 1951, *56*: 562–568.

Sklare, Marshall. "Intermarriage and the Jewish Future." *Commentary*, April 1964, 46–52.

Tinker, John N. "Intermarriage and Ethnic Boundaries: The Japanese American Case." *Journal of Social Issues*, 1973, *29*: 2, 49–66.

Thomas, John L. "The Factor of Religion in the Selection of Marriage Mates." *American Sociological Review*, 1951, *16*: 487–491.

U.S. Bureau of the Census. "Religion Reported by the Civilian Population of the United States: March 1957." *Current Population Reports*, Series P-20, No. 79 Washington, D.C.: U.S. Government Printing Office, 1958.

U.S. Bureau of the Census. "Perspectives on American Husbands and Wives." *Current Population Reports*, Series P-23, No. 77 Washington, D.C.: U.S. Government Printing Office, 1978.

Van Den Berghe, Peter L. "Hypergamy, Hypergenation, and Miscegenation."*Human Relations*, 1960, *13*: 1, 83–89.

Van Den Berghe, Peter L. "Racialism and Assimilation in Africa and the Americas." *Southwestern Journal of Anthropology*, 1963, *19*: 424–432.

Weinberger, Andrew D. "Interracial Intimacy: Interracial Marriage—Its Statutory Import, and Incidence." *Journal of Sex Research*, 1966, *2*: 3, 157–168.

Yamamoto, George K. "Interracial Marriage in Hawaii." *Interracial Marriage: Expectations and Realities*, Irving G. Stuart and Lawrence Edwin eds. New York: Grossman, 1973.
Zeleny, Carolyn. "Relations Between the Spanish-Americans and the Anglo-Americans in New Mexico." Ph.D. thesis, Yale University (unpublished), 1944.

BLACK-AMERICAN INTERMARRIAGE IN THE UNITED STATES

Ernest Porterfield

In order to maintain their cohesiveness and identity, many groups have explicit rules about who may marry whom. These constraints on intermarriage may be based on religious, political, cultural, social class, and/or racial-ethnic differences (Clayton, 1979:298). But the pressure to marry within one's race appears to be the strongest. Although changes have occurred over the past three decades, interracial marriage is still frowned on (Belkin and Goodman, 1980:187). Nothing would infuriate many white parents more than even the thought of their offspring marrying a black. No other mixture touches off such widespread condemnation as black-white race mixing.

As important as this issue is, information on interracial marriage in the United States has never been systematically collected. Therefore, determining the locations and frequency of black-white marriages is exceedingly difficult. Thus, knowledge of its nature, extent, and changing character is inadequate. For the first time, in 1960, the U.S. population census was tabulated to show the number of husbands and wives who had the same or different racial backgrounds. However, serious problems exist in regard to both the accuracy and the meaning of the census-assembled interracial figures (see Monahan, 1974:669-71). Information from public documents such as marriage and divorce records is fragmentary, geographically limited, ambiguous, and non-representative. Furthermore, because of repeated pressures accompanying the civil rights movement, currently there is a trend toward removal of racial identification from public records. And, even when available, in some areas, the publication of such is prohibited by law (Monahan, 1970:461-72). At any rate, let us take a brief look at trends based upon the available data.

Demographic Trends of Black-White Marriages

Currently, the national frequency of racial intermarriage is not known. Although many states collect marriage data, some gather no information on the race of the applicants. The United States Census publishes reports on the marital status of the population which include some data on mixed marriages. These data however, are estimates, based on a 5 percent sample which provides information on intermar-

Ernest Porterfield, PhD, is in the Department of Sociology, University of Alabama, Birmingham.

17

riage for the entire country and for several regions, but not for the separate states. The use of the small population samples magnifies this problem because selection tends to depend on availability rather than full knowledge of the universe. Although the National Center for Health Statistics (1970) reports on marriage occurrences which include certain racial data for selected states and areas, black-white intermarriage figures are not reported.

The earliest series of statistical data on black-white marriages were replete with historical incidents and case materials (Dubois, 1899; Hoffman, 1886, 1923; Baker, 1912; Reuter, 1918; Herbert, 1939; Davis, 1941; Merton, 1941; and Panunzio, 1942). Later, a set of data to come forth was based on marriage records, personal interviews, and psychiatric and social problem cases, and specific population censuses (Golden, 1951, 1953, 1959; Lynn, 1950, 1953, 1956, 1967; Risdon, 1954; Cash, 1956, Roberts, 1956; Barnett, 1963; Burma, 1952, 1963; Pavela, 1964; Heer, 1965, 1967,1974; Monahan,1966,1970a, 1971b, 1970b,1971b,1973; Cretser, 1967, Burma et al., 1970; and Porterfield, 1973, 1978). This information, as pointed out by Monahan (1970, 1976) enabled researchers to examine the social, psychological, and demographic characteristics of the interracially married.

Despite these limitations, the national frequency of racial intermarriage has been conservatively estimated at approximately 2,000 per year, or one in every 1,200 marriages. Figures are available for New York State and Boston for the early years of this century, for upstate New York from 1916 to 1964, and for California, Hawaii, Michigan, and Nebraska during the 1950s and 1960s. Figures for Boston after 1938 are unavailable (Jacobson, 1959:62). Table 1 provides a statistical summary of these trends from 1874-1937.

Monahan (1971:94-105) also examined intermarriage statistics in upstate New York from 1916 to 1964. From 1916 to 1921 the percent of mixed non-white and black marriages rose to a high point of 7.6 and 6.2 percent repectively. Thereafter, there was a gradual decline until 1950. An upward trend reasserted in 1951 with a dramatic rise from 1958 to 1964. Burma's (1963:156-165) study of interracial marriages in Los Angeles County from 1948 to 1959 revealed a significant increase. Some 3,200 were recorded, with black-white and Filipino-white marriages the most common. At the end of this eleven-year period, the rates were about triple of those at the beginning of this period.

Heer's (1966:262-273) analysis of the statistics for the 1950s and 1960s indicates that in only three states was there any officially published record of such intermarriages: Hawaii (1956-64), Michigan (1953-63), and Nebraska (1961-64). For selected years (1955,1957,1958, and 1958), the state of California made public a cross-tabulations of marriages by race of bride and groom. However, in the early 1960s, new legislation prohibited this practice. In all four states (for the period studied) the trend in recent years has been for a rise both in the proportion of white men marrying black women and of black men marrying white women.

Utilizing the published statistics for Hawaii, Monahan (1966:40-47) charted the distribution of interacial marriage from 1956 to 1962. Thirty seven percent of all marriages were intermarriages. These included black, Korean, Puerto Rican,

Table 1.   Summary of Earlier Studies of the Number of Black-White
           Intermarriages: 1874-1937

Researcher	Area	Period	Number of Inter-marriages	Average per Year
Hoffman	Michigan	1874-1893	111	5.5
Hoffman	Connecticut	1883-1893	65	5.9
Hoffman	Rhode Island	1883-1893	58	5.3
Hoffman	Boston	1855-1887	600	18.2
Dubois[a]	Philadelphia	1896-1897	33	----
Baker[b]	Boston	1899-1905	171	----
Wright	Philadelphia	1900	6	----
Stone	Boston	1900-1904	143	28.6
Stephenson	Boston	1900-1907	222	27.7
Wright	Philadelphia	1901-1904	21	5.2
Drachsler	New York City	1908-1912	52	10.4
Wirth and Goldhamer	Boston	1914-1938	276	5.4
DePorte	New York State	1919-1929	347	31.5
Wirth and Goldhamer[c]	New York State	1916-1937	569	----

SOURCES: Louis Wirth and Herbert Goldhamer, "The Hybrid and the Problem
of Miscegenation," in Otto Klineberg, ed., Characteristics of the American Negro
(New York: Harper and Row, 1944), p. 277.
[a]W. E. B. Dubois, The Philadelphia Negro: A Social Study (New York: Schocken,
1967), pp. 358-367. These findings are based on couples living in Philadelphia's
Seventh Ward only.
[b]Edward B. Reuter, The Mulatto in the United States (Boston: Gorham Press,
1918), p. 135.
[c]Exclusive of New York City.

Japanese, Filipino, Chinese, Hawaiian, and Caucasian. Thus, by piecing together
the earlier and later data, it may be tentatively concluded that the rate of black-white
intermarriage has been curvilinear, declining from the late 1900s to about 1940,
and rising gradually since that time. For example, in 1960, there was a total of
148,000 interracial marriages in existence. By 1970 the number had increased to
330,000 as shown in Table 2.

The 1977 total of interracial marriages was 421,000 (U.S. Bureau of the Census, 1978, p. 23, No. 77:7). Only a minority of this total consists of black-white
marriages. In 1960 there were 51,409 black-white marriages in existence; in 1970
the total black-white marriages in existence increased to 64,789 (see Table 3); and
by 1977 to 125,000. Nevertheless, today in 1981 less than one percent of all marriages are interracial (Reiss, 1980:333).

The Case for and Against Racial Endogamy

To many who are concerned with the civil rights of minority groups, traditional
American endogamy has often appeared as a kind of de facto nuptial segregation.
The fact that endogamy is prescribed and promoted by conservative moralists and
religionists often damns it by association, regardless of what actual merits it might
have. Some object to this pattern on the ground that a marriage based entirely on

Table 2.   Race of Husband by Race of Wife: 1970 U. S. A.

	RACE OF WIFE	
	White	Negro
Number by Race of Husband		
White . . .40,740,647	40,578,427	23,566
Negro . . . 3,393,555	41,223	3,334,292
Percent by race of Husband	100.00	100.0
White.	99.7	0.7
Negro.	0.1	99.2

SOURCE: U. S. Bureau of the Census; 1972.   1970 Census of Population PC(2)4c "Marital Status," Table 12, p. 262. Percents are rounded to the nearest tenth of one percent.

endogamous factor does not necessarily result in a happy union. Instead, it reinforces the anti-individualistic, anti-personal freedom bias of the American middle class. Although it results in accommodation to the status quo, it does not lead to the achievement of positive goals in marriage. One of the major arguments against endogamy is that there is an increasing number of people who are happily married to a partner of a different social class, religion, nationality/race. Despite the arguments, pro or con, there still exists a strong conflict in norms regarding the right of and individual to select a marriage partner irrespective of race (Klemer, 1970:110-112).

According to Goode (1980:8-16), since strong love attachments can occur in any society and are frequently a basis for and a prelude to marriage, they must be controlled. The importance of this situation may be seen clearly by considering one of the major functions of the family: status placement. The child's placement and choice of mates are socially important because both link two kinship lines together. Therefore, courtship or mate choice cannot be ignored. The family can disregard the question of who marries whom, only if a marriage is not seen as a link between kin lines and only if no property, power, lineage, honor, totemic relationships, are believed to flow from the kin through the spouses to their offspring. Universally, however, these are believed to follow kin lines. Thus, mate choice has consequences for the social structure.

In this connection, acute anxiety about black-white marriages is illustrated by nearly unanimous hesitation in opinion polls. For instance, 80 percent of the students questioned in American colleges and universities labeled interracial marriage the most difficult (compared to nine percent for interreligious or intereducational, four for international and, three percent for interclass marriage as measured by economic background (Gordon, 1964). Notwithstanding these polls, interracial dating is fairly common on many campuses and elsewhere. This does not, however, mean that much of it eventuates in marriage. According to one survey, almost one in five Americans has dated a member of another race (Downs,1971:56-57). Although disapproval of interracial marriage by adults still outweighs disapproval by teenagers (54 to 36 percent), the percentage of adults who approve almost doubled between 1968 and 1978, from 20 to 36 percent (Gallup, August 1978). In another survey, 52 percent of the teenagers approved of marriages between whites and blacks. A substantially higher percentage of nonwhite teenagers (76 percent) approve of interracial marriages (Gallup, April 1978). Granting studies indicate that attitudes toward racially mixed dating/marriages are fairly tolerant, actual behavior is a different matter (Melville, 1980:46).

Irrespective of the strong and widespread opposition, there has been an increase in interracial relationships. The 1954 Supreme Court's decision (Brown vs. Board of Education), the rising self-consciousness of blacks and the enactment of certain laws, particularly the Civil Rights Acts of 1964 and 1965, and the repeal of the anti-miscegenation laws in 1967 repudiated and dismantled the legal structure of segregation and separation (Degler, 1971:268). Another factor is the cause-and-effect

Table 3.   Number of Black-White Marriages by Type and Region, United States, 1960 and 1970

	1960	1970	Percentage Change Since 1960
United States:			
Total	51,409	64,798	+ 26.0
Husband black, wife white	25,496	41,223	+ 61.7
Husband white, wife black	25,913	23,566	− 9.1
North and West:			
Total	30,977	51,420	+ 66.0
Husband black, wife white	16,872	34,937	+107.1
Husband white, wife black	14,105	16,483	+ 16.9
South:			
Total	20,432	13,369	− 34.6
Husband black, wife white	8,624	6,286	− 27.1
Husband white, wife black	11,808	7,083	− 40.0

SOURCE: David M. Heer, "The Prevalence of black-white marriage in the United States, 1960 and 1970." Journal of Marriage and the Family 36: 246-258.

relationship between social change and acceptance of a phenomenon, which in turn facilitates its frequency. The more racial intermarriage occurs, the more it is likely to occur and be accepted (Bowman, 1965:207). Heer (1966:262-273) emphasizes an overall rise in the status of many blacks as a major factor for the increase in black-white unions. However, he does not feel there will be any dramatic increase in the rate of black-white marriages in the next 100 years.

Motives for Black-White Marriages

In spite of the strong taboo against it, what are the motives for black-white inter-marriage? Several theories have been proposed. The notion that those who contract mixed marriages are somehow different finds reinforcement in both popular and professional circles. This nonconformity varies from very mild to strong. A black psychiatrist asserted that "deep seated psychological sickness of various sorts underline the 'vast majority' of marriages between blacks and whites, and that these unions are arenas for hostility, control, and revenge" (Osmundsen, 1965:731). Another explanation is that some whites marry nonwhites for idealistic or liberal reason, i.e., to defy the prevalent cultural prejudice of society. Still another reason is the "lure of the exotic." The individual may experience a profound psycho-sexual attraction to the "otherness" of someone who may be physically different. There is also the notion that a white person may marry a nonwhite to rebel against parental authority (Saxton, 1968:332). A fifth motive is repudiation. Cavan (1969:206) asserts that a mixed marriage "indicates that the person either has not been thoroughly integrated into his/her social group or has repudiated it for some reason. Finally, the idea of neurotic self-hate or self-degradation (by marriage to an "inferior") also finds reinforcement in some circles (Rubenstein, 1963:112-142). The problem with most of these conceptual notions is that they are unsystematic, fragmentary, and speculative. In many instances, they are derived on the basis of individual cases or small samples. Therefore such information should not be accepted as a valid reason for all mixed marriages.

In view of the greater opportunities for increased contacts and interaction between different groups in recent years, many interracial marriages now occur simply because the individuals are in love. In these cases, there is no motivational difference between a conventional and an interracial marriage. A recent investigation by Potterfield (1978) which is based on a sample of 40 legally married black-white couples (33 black male/white female and seven white male/black female combinations) suggests that many black-white couples marry for the same reasons as do couples of the general population. A major limitation of this study, however, is that since no attempt was made to draw a representative sample, conclusions and inferences should not be interpreted as applying to the total black-white married population of the United States.

Motives for marriage in the study by Potterfield are classified into three general categories: (1) nonrace-related, (2) race-related, and (3) the marginal status of an individual in his/her racial group. Table 4 indicates the number of respondents who specifically mentioned different motives for marriage.

Table 4.   Number of Respondents Who Mentioned Specific Motives
            for Their Marriage

Motives	Race and Sex of Spouse			
	Black male	Black female	White male	White female
Nonrace-related motives				
Love	28	12	6	25
Compatibility	28	12	6	25
Pregnancy		1		1
Race-related motives				
Other race more appealing, interesting				2
Rebellion against society	3			
White female a "status symbol"	2			
White female less domineering	4			
Black female more independent, self-sufficient			1	
Marginality				
Desire for a husband of comparable educational-occupational status		2		
Ostracized from one's own racial group				1

Although these categories are mutually exclusive, motives for marriage
are not. Some of the respondents indicated a combination of reasons for
marriage.

Table 5 lists combinations of motives as reported by husband and wife. Grounds
for interracial marriages are usually the same as those for marriages between persons of the same race, i.e., love and compatibility, for example.

Albeit many unconventional social and psychological characteristics have been
ascribed to individuals marrying interracially, my data do not support this argument.
To the contrary, they strongly suggest that a majority of the interracial dating and
marriage on the part of these respondents is not related either to some pathological
abnormality or any crusade against prejudice. With few exceptions, this group's
motives for marriage do not appear to be any different from those individuals marrying "in the conventional style," i.e., within one's own race.

The Social Context of Black-White Marriages

Studies conducted between 1897-1964 indicate that black-white marriages more
often involved individuals who tended to be older than those who contracted racially
endogamous marriages. There is some evidence that these persons had been previously
married and were relatively isolated from their families. Often, the family and friends
of the white spouse did not know of the courtship, which tended to be carried on
with some secrecy. In some cases, this clandestineness was continued after marriage. As to the "social types," some of the blacks were intellectuals, bohemians,
members of cults, and lower-class and foreign-born. A few had lost their jobs when
employers learned of their marriages. Others concealed their marriages from
employers and fellow workers.

Some were discriminated against in securing housing. They usually lived in black

Table 5   Motives for Marriage Among Black-White Couples

Motives	Marital Combination	
	Black male-white female	White male-black female
Love and compatibility only	28	3
Love, compatibility and other motives		
1. H-Rebellion, and white female less domineering / W-Love-compatibility	1	
2. H-Rebellion, and white female a status symbol / W-Love-compatibility	1	
3. H-Love-compatibility / W-Love-compatibility, and pregnancy	1	2
4. H-Independency, self-sufficiency, & love-compatibility / W-Love-compatibility, and a desire to marry a person of comparable educational-occupational status		1
5. H-Love-compatibility / W-Love-compatibility, and a desire to marry a person of comparable educational-occupational status		1
Other combinations of motives (excluding love-compatibility)		
1. H-Rebellion, and white female less domineering / W-Other race more appealing-interesting	1	
2. H-White female a status symbol / W-Ostracized from own racial group	1	

H = Husband
W = Wife

communities or in peripheral areas. These marriages tended to be accepted by the black, but not by the white spouses' relatives and friends. On the other hand, not all of the white spouses' parents and relatives were opposed to such unions. Their friends were more often black than white; relatively few had extensive contacts with other interracially married couples. The problem of being stared at in public places was mentioned by several respondents. Most of the couples had children. Little discrimination against the children was generated from blacks, but virtually all parents acknowledged that their children would have to be reared as black. Some of the children suffered emotional and social maladjustment. A small number solved this dilemma by passing, while others made adjustments in the black community. In general, the problems encountered by interracial couples were those typically met by black couples.

Research since 1964 indicates that the secretiveness previously associated with black-white dating is declining. As in the past, however, a majority of the weddings in the Porterfield investigation continued to be performed with little publicity and with a small number of persons in attendance. Most families reported being relatively happy. Their problems are no different from those of any other marriage. Quarrels seldom carry racial overtones. Most of the parents feel their children will not encounter insurmountable discriminatory problems. A few families, however, do not concur with this opinion. Many of the respondents' kinsmen oppose these marriages. Despite some couples having been married for several years, most of the white parents and relatives have changed neither their negative position nor their attitudes. On the other hand, the kinsmen of a majority of the black spouses are more receptive to mixed marriages.

It is not surprising that strong norms against racial intermarriage should be accompanied by beliefs that such marriages are fraught with special hazards and are more likely to fail than are racially homogamous marriages. However, except for some nonconfirming information from the state of Hawaii, in recent years, nothing is known statistically to support this thesis of instability (Monahan, 1966:40-47). As Kephart (1961:607) says, "No divorce statistics are available which would enable us to generalize about their instability." Moreover, Monahan's (1970:461-473) analysis of a small set of data (published and unpublished records) on the state of Iowa for 1940-67, indicates the divorce rate for black-black couples to be about twice as high as that for whites. But black-white marriages are more stable than black-black, and black husbands and white wives have a lower divorce outcome than do white couples.

It appears that black communities are divided on the issue of interracial marriage. Some blacks view this phenomenon as one channel through which equality can be achieved. Others feel that at this point, for a black to marry across the "color line" is inconsistent with a developing sense of a black peoplehood. The general atmosphere appears to be one of acceptance by a majority in black communities, toleration by others, and total rejection by a minority. Many black females and older blacks are the most vehement opponents. The large national surplus of black women to black men may explain the loudest protest by the former. Younger black males tend to express apathy regarding these unions.

In regards to housing and employment, some gains have been made within the last two decades. These couples now live in all types of neighborhoods—with a slight majority in either all black or on the periphery of predominantly all white communities. Some are discriminated against in their efforts to obtain housing; some are not. Housing seems to be less of a problem if the wife is black. Some overt hostility toward mixed families exists in both black and white communities. The least amount appears in public apartment complexes.

A majority of these families have had no difficulties in the area of employment. However, a small number reported losing their jobs because of their marriage. Today, mixed couples are less secretive about revealing their marital status to employers. For example, a few even informed their employers before being hired. In no case did this prove to be detrimental. The current trend is that service institutions in general are more liberal regarding the treatment of black-white couples. It is unlikely that this trend will reverse in the future.

Trends in Black-White Marital Combinations

Merton (1941:361-374) observed that intermarriage does not occur at random but according to more or less two patterns: *hypergamy,* wherein the female marries into a higher social stratum; and *hypogamy,* in which she marries into a lower stratum. Although many research findings indicate that hypogamy (marriage between black males and white females) exceeds hypergamy (white males and black females), there is a lack of consensus on this point as well as on the explanations for the difference (U.S. Department of Health, Education, and Welfare, 1971:20; Eshleman, 1974:316). An investigation of a summary of *empirical* studies of the amount of black-white intermarriage from 1874 to 1970 for the country as a whole and nine states (Michigan, Rhode Island, Massachusetts, New York, California, Indiana, Hawaii, Nebraska, and Wisconsin) and for nine cities (Boston, New York, Philadelphia, Washington, D.C., Los Angeles, Champaign-Urbana, Ill., Cambridge, Ohio, Birmingham, Al., and Jackson, Ms.), reveals a preponderance of hypogamous unions. Table 6 reports these findings.

The marital pattern which appears to be more pronounced for any given period depends upon the source of the data and how it is analyzed. When the census data are analyzed on the basis of: *year husband first married* (i.e., when the husband was marrying for the first time), from before 1940 up to 1949, there were slightly more hypergamous marriages with an almost one to one ratio. But when we analyze it from the standpoint of: *when both partners were marrying for the first time,* from 1940 up to 1970, there is a geater tendency toward hypogamous unions. Table 7 describes these trends from before 1940 to 1960. Table 8 reports these figures from 1940 to 1970.

The national data from the Bureau of the Census on black-white marital combinations are inconsistent with data derived from *empirical studies.* For no period in the history of this country has any empirical study reflected a preponderance of hypergamous marriages. By and large, they are extremely hypogamous. Only from before 1940 until 1949 did the *census* report a slightly overall greater hypergamous tendency *in which the husband was marrying for the first time.* The trend, however, reversed during the 1950-1960 decade, i.e., with a hypogamous orientation (see Table 8).

Two earlier explanations have been advanced for the more widespread hypogamous pattern. One is the socioeconomic status of the black male. If these marriages involve black men of high and white women of low social status, an exchange is in operation in that the black male offers his higher socioeconomic position for the preferred color-caste of the lower class white female. The second explanation is the *accessibility hypothesis.* Black men simply have not had social access to white women. Moreover, social and sexual overtures from black men directed at white women—for the most part—have been prohibited either by law or custom or both.

Aside from the investigation by Porterfield (1978), research conducted since the 1960s does not support the first explanation. The evidence suggests that, currently,

Table 6. Summary of Empirical Studies of the Number of Black-White Intermarriages by Sex and Color of Marriage Partners, 1874-1965

Researcher	Area	Period	Number of black male-white female	Number of white male-black female	% Black male-white female of all black-white marriages	% White male-black female of all black-white marriages
Hoffman	Michigan	1874-1893	93	18	84	16
Hoffman	Rhode Island	1883-1893	51	7	88	12
Stone	Massachusetts[a]	1900	43	9	83	17
Stone	Boston	1900-1904	133	10	93	7
Stephenson	Boston	1900-1907	203	19	91	9
Drachsler	New York City	1908-1912	41	11	79	21
DePorte	New York State[b]	1919-1929	262	85	76	25
Wirth and Goldhamer	Boston	1914-1938	227	49	82	18
Wirth and Goldhamer	New York State[b]	1916-1937	424	145	75	26
Golden	Philadelphia	1922-1947	24	17	59	41
Lynn	Washington D. C.	1940-1947	19	7	73	27
Burma	Los Angeles	1948-1959	800	267	75	25
Barnett	California	1955-1959	921	252	78	22
Pavela	Indiana	1958-1959	72	19	69	31
U. S. Census	U. S.	1960	25,496	25,913	50	50
Heer	Michigan	1953-1963	862	267	76	24
Heer	Hawaii	1956-1964	59	15	80	20
Heer	Nebraska	1961-1964	6	2	75	25
Heer	Wisconsin	1964	38	5	88	12
Annella	Washington D. C.	1931-1965	523	295	62	38
Porterfield[d]	Champaign-Urbanna, Ill.; Cambridge, Ohio; B'ham, Al.; Jackson, Ms.	1970	523	7	05	01

a 57 Towns and Cities   b Exclusive of New York City

SOURCES: Louis Wirth and Herbert Goldhamer, "The Hybrid and the Problem of Miscegenation," in Otto Klineberg, ed., Characteristics of the American Negro (New York: Harper and Row, 1944), p. 277.
aW.E.B. DuBois, The Philadelphia Negro: A Social Study (New York: Schocken, 1967), pp. 358-367. These findings are based on couples living in Philadelphia's Seventh Ward only.
bEdward B. Reuter, The Mulatto in the United States (Boston: Gorham Press, 1918), p. 135.   cExclusive of New York City.
dErnest Porterfield, Black and White Mixed Marriages: An Ethnographic Study of Black-White Families (Chicago, Nelson-Hall, 1978).

Table 7.   Black–White Marriages in the United States by Decade in
                Which Only the Husband Was Marrying for the First Time.

Decade	Totals	Black male– white female	White male– black female
Before 1940	20,568	9,291	11,277
1940–1949	13,531	6,613	6,918
1950–1960	17,310	9,592	7,718
Totals	51,409	25,496	25,913

SOURCES: U. S. Department of Commerce, Bureau of the Census, United
States Census of Population: 1960, Subject Report, Marital Status,
Report PC (2)-4E, pp. 160–161.

Table 8.   Black–White Marriages in the United States by Decade in
                Which Both Partners Were Marrying for the First Time

Decade	Totals	Black male– white female	White male– black female
1940–1949	4,548	2,267	2,281
1950–1959	7,622	4,780	2,842
1960–1970*	23,771	16,419	7,352
Totals	35,941	23,466	12,475

*The total number of mixed married couples in 1970 irrespective of the
number of times married was 64,789, of which 41,223 consisted of black men
and white women and 23,566 of white men and black women.
    SOURCE: U. S. Department of Commerce, Bureau of the Census, United
States Census of Population: 1970, Subject Report, Marital Status, Report
PC (2), pp. 262–263.

individuals who contract a black-white marriage tend to be similar (homogamous)
with respect to social, educational, and occupational characteristics. The *accessibility
hypothesis* seems to be more effective in explaining the preponderance of black males
(than does the exchange theory) because in such cases, due to societal pressures,
these men were more or less forced to legitimize their sexual liaisons with white
women through marriage. This was not the case with respect to white males in their
relations with black females.

Some factors which probably facilitated the development of this hypogamous
pattern are (1) black men rebelling against white society, (2) black men's percep-
tion that the white woman is a status symbol, (3) the idea that the white female
is less domineering than her black counterpart, (4) physically, the white female is
considered to be more beautiful than most other American females, and (5) permanent availability, i.e., the opportunity for any person of age to marry any other individual irrespective of race, color, creed, or national origin. Reiss (1980:333-335)
also notes that it is possible that a higher proportion of black males compared to
black females attend predominantly white colleges and if so, this might partially
explain the hypogamous pattern. Also, it is likely that white females and black males
have more favorable attitudes toward the other race than do their counterparts.

However, these are purely hunches and should be examined along with other explanations.

Intermarriage and Mate Selection: Some Theoretical Points of View

According to Merton (1941:361-374), one of the problems in studying black-white marriages in the United States is the lack of a broad theoretical framework. He sees rates and patterns of intermarriage as being related to cultural orientations, income and symbols of status; and asserts that the conflicts and accommodations of mates from socially disparate groups are partly understandable in terms of this structure. While this model served to stimulate research, the findings did not always support Merton's hypotheses. Even in recent times, there has been no development of an integrated theory of interracial marriage. I attempt to modify this current state of "theory," by integrating Merton's ideas of rules of endogamy with the notion of "restricted and generalized patterns of exchange" (alliance and descent theories), and the concepts of orderly replacement vs. permanent availability." Aside from the exchange theory and the accessibility hypothesis (previously discussed) "frames of reference" should provide additional insight for studying the dynamics of black-white marriages.

Restricted and Generalized Exchange

In the study of kinship organization, researchers have made extensive use of two theoretical frameworks: the "alliance" and "descent" approaches. Alliance theory assumes that kinship structures derive from the regulation of marital exchange. Descent theory is concerned with rules or devices that preserve the continuity of the lineage. These theoretical viewpoints are complementary rather than conflicting (Fox, 1967:235).

Levi-Strauss (1969) views kinship systems as methods of organizing marriage relations between groups and as simply being units in a system of "alliances" made or "expressed" by marriage. In marital transactions, people represent a commodity, i.e., property. Some of the group's most important assets are its wives and daughters. The descent model views kinship systems as mechanisms for the formation and recruitment of property owning, residential, and political groups, etc. This "genetic" (restricted exchange) model conceptualizes the integration of groups as based on their real or assumed common ancestry (Fox, 1967:228).

Elementary systems are concerned with "exchange and alliance." Once an alliance has been formed, it is perpetuated, i,e., once two groups have exchanged women, they continue to do so. This defines the category of persons whom one may not as well as must marry. The systems differ in the ways in which they organize marriage rules. This implies two alternatives: as far as any unit is concerned, its "wife givers" are either the same as its "wife takers," or they are different. If they are the same, then this involves the principle of "straight swaps." If they are different, then women are not being directly exchanged but instead circulated around the system. Lévi-Strauss has characterized the first kind of system as "restricted exchange" and the second as "generalized exchange." Exchange is "restricted" where it has to include two groups who exchange directly. This might suit small populations. The "generalized" method on the other hand, can expand indefinitely.

Generally, property may be regarded as something which may be withheld or prohibited from exchange. Property then is nonreciprocal. Oftentimes, situations exist in which a kin group does not want to establish a co-operative relationship with another group. In American society, religious and racial intermarriage is often discouraged on this basis (Farber, 1971:12-14). Heer (1966:262-273) also observes that restriction on racial intermarriage may be closely linked to economic discrimination. On a per capita basis, whites hold a far higher share of wealth than do blacks. The formal and informal prohibitions on intermarriage serve to perpetuate this pattern of inequality, since it is unlikely that blacks will inherit wealth from whites. A relaxation of the norms militating against miscegenation, then, might have a significant and crucial effect on the socioeconomic position of black Americans.

In Great Britain, patterns of marital mobility are also changing. The English aristocracy, while being largely endogamous, has nevertheless "married down" a good deal. While it is hard to compare Western with primitive societies, one can easily look at them as a variant on the alliance theme and ask how women (and men for that matter) are distributed around the system through marriage, and what are the directions and intensities of these flows. Fox (1967:238-239) notes that if we are looking for the channels along which alliances may flow, then we move into this wider sociological perspective which may give new insights into the dynamics of our own society.

Order Replacement vs. Permanent Availability

Bernard Farber (1964:103-186) suggests a theory which also helps to understand the hypogamous nature of black-white marriages. The family, he says, should be regarded in terms of a lineage system or "orderly replacement" and availability of individuals for marriage—"permanent availability." If orderly replacement is to occur, each family of orientation must provide for the continuance of its values and norms relating to patterns of family life and the socialization of children. Each family then serves to transmit cultural patterns.

In industrialized societies, lineage considerations in mate selection are at a minimum and kinship control over marriage dissipates. As a result, individuals become available for marriage with anyone at any time during their adulthood. Thus, in urbanized systems, a greater tendency probably exists for people to marry outside their particular cultural complex, and in some instances their racial context. This being the case naturally enlarges one's field of eligibles which are likely to include members of minority groups. Once these endogamous prescriptions are relaxed, unlike males of the dominant group who have always been permitted to make sexual advances toward minority group women, minority group males are likely to initiate similar relationships with women of the dominant group-which more often are legitimated through marriage.

Intermarriage is on the increase not only because of a breakdown in parental control over mate selection but also because the traditional social categories which define intermarriage are themselves becoming vague and diffuse. As the various segments of the population lose their visibility, barriers to intermarriage are dissolved. In spite of the tendency for old categories to persist, other categories of mate selection such as personal characteristics will likely increase in relative importance. These factors contribute even more to the hypogamous tendency.

Conclusion

The gradual integration of minority groups into the main steam of American life has increased contact between groups and is therefore decreasing the social and economic obstacles which previously separated them. Also, since laws against interracial marrige were declared unconstitutional by a United States Supreme Court decision in June 1967, it is likely that all types of mixed marriages will continue to increase in the near future. However, there is still much opposition to intermarriage.

Many whites no doubt will continue to exploit the fear of black-white marriage as a basis for rationalizing retention of economic superiority. Moreover, even the possibility of its occurrence, given the implication of black-white equality inherent in such a union may be preceived as having devastating consequences. It may be necessary, then, that blacks devise an ordered set of theoretical constructs under which a strategy to attack racism can be developed. The notion of a "symbolic family estate" (i.e., the development of a black peoplehood) might achieve this end. Black awareness will have some negative effect on the rate of black-white marriages, but it is my guess, that if there is a decrease, it will be slight and only for a short period of time. One reason is that through the development of a "symbolic family estate," blacks will increasingly achieve a higher status. For it is only through the achievement and the realization of this complete selfhood can the black man exercise greater control of his destiny.

Future black-white marriages will have a more congenial climate for success as society continues to become more attuned to individual freedom and personal rights regardless of race, color, creed, or religion. Social scientists can also play a vital role in improving conditions (for the interracially married) by objectively analyzing this phenomenon so that many of the myths, misconceptions, and underlying principles of failure are put to rest. Such studies would not necessarily facilitate an increase in interracial marriages, but would certainly provide a healthier climate for those who choose to enter such a relationship.

Black-white marriage then should have a temendous impact upon race relations in the United States. It is relatively unimportant as to whether the incidence of these alliances increases or remains the same, but it is of much concern to many individuals that these unions are approved by a larger society. It is my conviction that the degree of acceptance of this phenomenon is a valuable index for measuring the extent to which a group is achieving social, economic, and political equality. If complete acceptance comes to pass, it is likely that discrimination in the United States based on race or skin color will cease to exist.

REFERENCES

Barnett, Larry D. "Research on international and interracial marriages." *Marriage and Family Living* 25:105–107, 1963. (a)

Barnett, Larry D. "Interracial marriage in California." *Marriage and Family Living* 25:424–427, 1963. (b)

Baker, Ray S. *Following the Color Line*. New York: Doubleday, 1912.

Belkin, Gary S. and Norman Goodman. *Marriage, Family and Intimate Relationships*. Chicago: Rand McNally, 1980.

Bowman, Henry A. *Marriage for Moderns*. New York: McGraw-Hill, 1965.

Burma, John H. "Research note on the measurement of interracial marriage." *American Journal of Sociology* 57:587–589, 1952.

Burma, John H. "Interethnic marriage in Los Angeles, 1948–1959." *Social forces* 42:156–165, 1963.

Burma, John, and Gary A. Cretser, and Ted Seacrest. "A comparison of the occupational status of intramarrying and intermarrying couples: 'A research note'." *Sociology and Social Research* 54:508–519, 1970.

Cash, Eugene. "A study of Negro-white marriages in the Philadelphia area." Unpublished doctoral dissertation, Temple University, 1956.

Cavan, Ruth S. *The American Family*. New York: Thomas Y. Crowell, 1969.

Clayton, Richard R. *The Family, Marriage, and Social Change*. Lexington, MA:D. C. Heath, 1979.

Cretser, Gary A. "An investigation of interethnic marriages in Los Angeles County, 1950–1961, and its relation to selected demographic factors." Unpublished master's thesis, University of Southern California, 1976.

Davis, Kingsley. "Intermarriage in cast societies." *American Anthropologist* 43:388–395, 1941.

Degler, Carl N. *Neither Black nor White*. New York: MacMillan, 1971.

Downs, Joan. "Black/White Dating." *Life* May 28:56–57, 1971.

Dubois, W. E. B. *The Philadelphia Negro: A Social Study*. New York: Schocken, 1967.

Eshleman, J. Ross. *The Family: An Introduction*. Boston: Allyn and Bacon, 1974.

Farber, Bernard. *Family: Organization and Interaction*. San Francisco: Chandler, 1964.

Farber, Bernard. *Kinship and Class: A Midwestern Study*. New York: Basic Books, 1971.

Fox, Robin. *Kinship and Marriage*. Baltimore: Penguin, 1967.

Gallup, George. "Interfaith/Interracial marriages acceptable to many teens." Gallup Youth Survey—Press Release: April 12, 1978. (a)

Gallup, George. "Dramatic changes in white viewpoints on integration and intermarriage." The Gallup Poll. Press Release: August 28, 1978. (b)

Goode, William J. "The theoretical importance of live." Pp. 8–16 in James M. Hemslin (ed.), *Marriage and Family in a Changing Society*. New York: Free Press, 1980.

Golden, Joseph. "Negro-white marriage in Philadelphia." Unpublished doctoral dissertation, University of Pennsylvania, 1951.

Golden, Joseph. "Characteristics of the Negro-white intermarried in Philadelphia." *American Sociological Review* 18:177–183, 1953.

Golden, Joseph. "Facilitating factors in Negro-white intermarriage." *Phylon* 20:273–284, 1959.

Gordon, Albert I. *Intermarrriage*. Boston: Beacon, 1964.

Heer, David M. "Negro-white marriages in the United States." *New Society* 6:7–9, 1965.

Heer, David M. "Negro-white marriage in the United States." *Journal of Marriage and the Family* 27:262–273, 1966.

Heer, David M. "Intermarriage and racial amalgamation in the United States." *Eugenics Quarterly* 14:112–120, 1967.

Heer, David M. "The Prevalence of Black-white marriage in the United States, 1960 and 1970." *Journal of Marriage and the Family* 36:246–258 and 36:671–672, 1974.

Herbert, Leona A. "A study of ten cases of Negro-white marriages in the Dictrict of Columbia." Unpublished M. A. Thesis, Catholic University of America, 1939.

Hoffman, Frederick L. *Racial Traits and Tendencies of the American Negro*. New York: Macmillan, 1896.

Hoffman, Frederick L. "The problem of Negro-white intermixture and intermarriage." Publications of the Second International Congress of Eugenics 2:175–188, 1923.

Jacobson, Paul H. *American Marriage and Divorce*. New York: Holt, Rinehart, and Winston, 1959.

Klemer, Richard H. *Marriage and Family Relationships*. New York: Harper and Row, 1970.

Lévi-Strauss, Claude. *The Elementary Structures of Kinship*. Boston: Beacon, 1969.

Lynn, Ann Q. "Interracial Marriage: A study of fifteen Negro-white marriages in New York City and the metropolitan area." Unpublished M.A. thesis, Catholic University of America, 1950.

Lynn, Ann Q. "Interracial marriages in Washington, D.C., 1940–1947." Ph.D. dissertation, Catholic University of America, 1953.

Lynn, Ann Q. "Some aspects of interracial marriage in Washington, D.C." *Journal of Negro Education* 25:380–391, 1956.

Lynn, Ann Q. "Interracial marriages in Washington, D.C." *Journal of Negro Education* 36:428–433, 1967.

Melville, Keith. *Marriage and Family Today*. New York: Random House, 1980.

Merton, Robert K. "Intermarriage and the social structure: Fact and theory." *Psychiatry* 4:361–374, 1941.

Monahan, Thomas P. "Interracial marriage and divorce in the state of Hawaii." *Eugenics Quarterly* 13:40–47, 1966.

Monahan, Thomas P. "Are interracial marriages really less stable? *Social Forces* 48:461–473, 1970. (a)

Monahan, Thomas P. "Interracial marriage: Data for Philadelphia and Pennsylvania." Demography 7:287–299, 1970. (b)

Monahan, Thomas P. "Interracial marriage in the United States: Some data on upstate New York." *International Journal of Sociology of the Family* 1:94–106, 1971. (a)

Monahan, Thomas P. "Interracial marriage and divorce in Kansas and the question of instability of mixed marriages." *Journal of Comparative Family Studies* 2:107–120, 1971. (b)

Monahan, Thomas P. "Marriage across racial lines in Indiana." *Journal of Marriage and the Family* 35:632–640, 1973.

Monahan, Thomas P. "Critique of Heer's article." *Journal of Marriage and the Family* 36:669–671, 1974.

Monahan, Thomas P. "An overview of statistics on interracial marriages in the United States, with data on its extent from 1963–1970." *Journal of Marriage and the Family* 38:223–231, 1976.

National Center for Health Statistics. Vital Statistics of the United States, 1970, Vol. II, Marriage and Divorce. Washington, D.C.: Government Printing Office, 1970.

Osmundsen, John A. "Doctor discusses mixed marriages." *New York Times*, Nov.: 731, 1965.

Panunzio, Constantine. "Intermarriage in Los Angeles, 1924–1933." *American Journal of Sociology* 47:690–701, 1942.

Pavela, Todd H. "An exploratory study of Negro-white intermarriage in Indiana." *Journal of Marriage and the Family* 26:209–211, 1964.

Porterfield, Ernest. "Mixed marriages." *Psychology Today* 6:71–78, 1973.

Porterfield, Ernest. *Black and White Mixed Marriages: An Ethnographic Study of Black-White Families*. Chicago: Nelson-Hall, 1978.

Reiss, Ira L. *Family Systems in America*. Holt, Rinehart and Winston, 1980.

Risdon, Randall. "A study of interracial marriages based on data for Los Angeles County." *Sociology and Social Research* 39:92–95, 1954.

Roberts, Robert E. T. "Negro-white intermarriage: A study of social control." Unpublished M. A. thesis, University of Chicago, 1940.

Roberts, Robert E. T. "A comparative study of social stratification and intermarriage in multiracial societies." Unpublished doctoral dissertation. University of Chicago, 1956.

Rubenstein, Richard L. "Intermarriage and conversion on the American College Campus." Pp. 122–142 in Werner J. Cahnman, (ed.), *Intermarriage and Jewish Life*. New York: Herzl, 1963.

Reuter, Edward B. *The Mulatto in the United States*. Boston: Gorham Press, 1918.

Reuter, Edward B. *Race Mixture: Studies in Intermarriage and Miscegenation*. New York: McGraw-Hill, 1931.

Saxton, Lloyd. *The Individual, Marriage, and the Family*. Belmont, CA: Wadsorth, 1968.

U.S. Bureau of the Census 1972. Census of Population PC(2)4C "Marital Status." Washington, D.C.: Government Printing Office, 1970.

U.S. Bureau of the Census. "Perspective on American Husbands and Wives." *Current Population Reports*. Series P–23, No. 77 (December). Washington, D.C.: Government Printing Office, 1978.

U.S. Department of Commerce, Bureau of the Census. U.S. Census of Population: 1960, Subject Report, Marital Status, Report PC(2)4E: 160–161, 1960.

U.S. Department of Commerce, Bureau of the Census. United States Census of Population: 1970, Subject Report, Marital Status, Report PC(2): 262–263, 1970.

U.S. Department of Health, Education and Welfare. "Marriages: Trends and Characteristics," United States, Series 21. Washington, D.C.: Government Printing Office. (September): 20, 1971.

Wirth, Louis, and Herbert Goldhamer. "The hybrid and the problem of miscegenation. Pp. 249–370 in Otto Klineberg (ed.), *Characteristics of the American Negro*. New York: Harper and Row, 1944.

CHINESE INTERRACIAL MARRIAGE

Harry H.L. Kitano
Wai-tsang Yeung

The Chinese were the earliest Asian group to immigrate to the United States so that there are some who can trace their American ancestry back four or five generations. Conversely, there has also been a continuing new migration, therefore others have literally just stepped off the plane. These differences are important in understanding the marital patterns of the Chinese, for the children of the oldtimers will have expectations and behaviors that will set them apart from the newcomers.

The purpose of this paper is to present data on the inmarriage and outmarriage patterns of the Chinese in the United States. Since nationwide data is extremely limited, we have chosen to present data on marital statistics for the Chinese in Los Angeles County for the years 1979, 1977, and 1975. Data on ethnic marriages was kept systematically up to 1959 when civil rights legislation prohibited racial identification. Since that time data on interracial marriages has been difficult to obtain.

Background

The background of the Chinese in the Americas can be traced back as early as the Ming Dynasty (1368–1644) and the Manila Galleons that sailed between Mexico and the Phillippines in the 16th century. Lai (1980:218) mentions the development of a Chinese colony in Mexico City in 1635.

The first major immigration of Chinese to the United States mainland took place between 1850 and 1882. More than 322,000 Chinese (including reentrants), primarily males, entered the country. The majority were unskilled laborers and peasants from the southern provinces of Fukien and Kwangtung. The majority came with a sojourners orientation so that they expected to make money in the new country and return to their homeland in style. Many of these immigrants were already married, but they often left their wives and children behind so that the early Chinese population consisted primarily of bachelors. As one consequence, the "Chinatowns" in which they lived were developed for the needs of a single, male community (Lai, 1980:221).

Harry H.L. Kitano, Ph.D., is affiliated with the Departments of Social Welfare and Sociology, U.C.L.A. Wai-tsang Yeung is a Graduate Student in the Department of Social Welfare, U.C.L.A. The authors wish to thank the Ford Foundation, the Institute of American Cultures, and the Asian American Studies Center at UCLA for funding the research.

This early group was subjected to racism and discrimination. A series of discriminatory laws culminated in the Chinese Exclusion Act of 1882 which forbade further Chinese immigration. Chinese were legally excluded from immigrating from 1882 to 1943. The effect of the various exclusion acts can be seen in the Chinese population figures as reported by the United States Census: there was a high of 107,488 in 1890 to a low of 61,639 in 1920.

The Chinese Exclusion Act was repealed in 1943 (China was on the side of the allies during World War II) and China was assigned a token quota of 110. Of more importance for family life was the admittance of wives as non-quota immigrants, so that female migrants vastly outnumbered the male migrants in the years from 1943 to 1970.

The end of the Chinese Civil War between the Communists and the Nationalists in 1949 brought about another type of immigration. The conflict created a large number of refugees, including members of the intelligentsia, upper classes, and families with wealth, many who ended up in the United States. There were also a number of Chinese students studying in the United States who were afraid of returning to their homeland because of the changes in the political system and were thereby granted immigrant status. These groups were quite different from the peasant laborers who had pioneered the initial Chinese migration.

The most recent migration has been the result of the 1965 Immigration Act which abolished national origin quotas. There has been steady flow of newcomers that continues to the present day. It is interesting to note that despite their long history in the United States, the 1970 census shows that of the 433,469 Chinese, 204,232 or 47 percent were foreign born.

Marital Patterns

There are a number of factors that have to be taken into account when dealing with Chinese-American marital patterns. The early arrivals were primarily young males, some already married. Prejudice and discrimination forced the majority into segregated Chinatowns where opportunities for contact with non- Chinese females were extremely limited. California miscegenation laws were enacted in 1850 and prohibited the marriage of Caucasians with Asians, Filipinos, Indians, and Negroes (Risdon, 1954:92). These laws were overturned in 1948.

A study by Barnett (1963) provides Chinese interracial marriage figures for California for the years 1955 through 1959 (see Table 1).

The Chinese outmarriage rates remained relatively consistent for the years measured. The lowest outmarriage rate was 14 percent in 1955 while the highest outmarriage rates were 17.9 percent in 1959.

Burma (1963) studied interracial marriages in Los Angeles County for the years 1948–1959 and found that the male Chinese outmarriage rate was 5.83 percent and the female outmarriage was 4.94 percent. The most common partnerships were between whites and Chinese.

Hawaii's pattern of interracial marriages probably reflects the more tolerant racial

Table 1

Chinese Outmarriage Rates by Sex
in California, for 1959, 1958, 1957, 1955

	Total Marriages	Inmarriage N	Percent	Outmarriage N	Percent
1959	431	354	82.1	77	17.9
1958	450	379	84.2	71	15.8
1957	432	359	83.1	73	16.9
1955	400	344	86.0	56	14.0

Source: Barnett, Larry, "Interracial Marriage in California", Marriage and Family Living, Nov. 1963, p. 425.

climate of the area. The early Chinese male immigrants were without Chinese females so that some married local Hawaiian women, others sent for brides, and a large number never married. In 1977, 64.7 percent of the Chinese married non-Chinese (Char et al., 1980) with the highest proportion of outmarriages to Japanese (26.1%), followed by the Caucasicans (20.7%). It should be emphasized that although there are new immigrants from Hong Kong and Taiwan, the great majority of Hawaii's Chinese are descendants of the approximately 50,000 pioneers who came to the Islands between 1852–1898.

Nationwide statistics based on the 1970 U.S. Census using the category "married with husband or wife of the same race" is shown on Table II.

The Chinese total outmarriage rate for the country was 13.5 percent for males and 12.3 percent for females. The highest outmarriage rates were in Hawaii (30.6 percent for males, 29.7 percent for females); the lowest in the state of New York (7.3 percent for males, 2.7 percent for females).

In summary, the available data indicates high rates of Chinese outmarriage in Hawaii and lower rates on the mainland. The data are limited to male and female differences and the discrepancies between the studies appear to be based primarily on the time span used (i.e., the U.S. Census is cumulative so that all married individuals are counted no matter what year they married, whereas other studies count the number of marriages in a specific year).

The Present Study

The present study focuses on the marital patterns of Chinese who married in Los Angeles County in 1979, 1977, and 1975. We checked the marriage application index and drew out every Chinese surname (as well as Japanese and Korean names). The surname, the birthplace of the applicant and the applicant's parents, as well as

Table II

Chinese Male and Female Marriages With Spouse of the
Same Race by Total and Selected States, 1970

1970				
Total U.S.	Married	Spouse of the Same Race	Percent Inmarried	Outmarried
Male	87,324	75,500	86.5	13.5
Female	85,415	74,903	87.7	12.3
California				
Male	33,973	30,858	90.8	9.2
Female	33,561	30,562	91.1	8.9
Hawaii				
Male	11,086	7,692	69.4	30.6
Female	10,845	7,625	70.3	29.7
Illinois				
Male	2,802	2,495	89.0	11.0
Female	2,784	2,471	88.8	11.2
Massachusetts				
Male	2,710	2,434	89.8	10.2
Female	2,578	2,370	92.0	8.0
New York				
Male	17,254	15,993	92.7	7.3
Female	16,534	15,927	96.3	3.7

Source: U.S. Census, Japanese, Chinese and Filipinos in the United States,
1970, pp. 76-82.

the name of the father and mother provided clues as to nationality. The research team
included individuals familiar with Asian surnames.

There are a number of Chinese names that can be confused as Caucasian (Yeung
or Yang may sometimes be spelled Young; Li for Lee); others with Korean surnames.
However, the birthplace of parents usually provided accurate clues as to nationality. We had no way of identifying those Asians who had changed their names or of
children of mixed marriages whose names were non-Asian. Any marriage with one
non-Chinese surname was considered an outmarriage. We can think of no systematic
bias in our gathering of data that would alter our findings.

Findings

Chinese Inmarriage and Outmarriage

1. Total and sex. Table III shows the in and outmarriage rates for the Chinese
by total and by sex for 1975, 1977, and 1979. Total outmarriage rates were as follows:
1975, 44 percent; 1977, 49.6 percent, and 1979, 41 percent. Outmarriage rates for

Chinese males was 1975, 37.8 percent, 1977, 43.8 percent, and 1979, 44 percent. Outmarriage rates for Chinese females was 1975, 62.2 percent; 1977, 56.2 percent, and 1979, 56 percent.

The current outmarriage rates are substantially higher than the rates reported by Burma (1963) for Los Angeles County in the 1950s. His study found that for 1948–1959, the Chinese male outmarriage rate was 5.83 percent and the female outmarriage rate was 4.94 percent. Part of the reason for the higher outmarriage rate of the males could be attributed to the Chinese male to female ratio where the 1960 census reported 10,836 males to 8,450 females in Los Angeles County.

2. Ethnicity of the non-Chinese spouse. Table IV shows that of the 293 outmarriages, 77 were to other Asians, primarily Japanese, while 216 were to non-Asians. Therefore, if we exclude the 64 Japanese and 13 Koreans from the outmarried category, the rate of interracial marriage in 1979 drops to 30.2 percent. For 1977 the interracial marriage rate drops to 39.7 percent, and for 1975, 33.2 percent.

3. Age. The age categories of the male and female Chinese is shown on Table V. The outmarried male was higher in the under 25 category (35.7 percent) in comparison to the inmarried male (20.0 percent), while the inmarried male predominated in the 26–30 and 31–40 year old age range. The chi-square of 16.67 comparing the inmarried and outmarried male by age was statistically significant.

In terms of mean age the differences were as follows: outmarried male, 1979, 29.4 years; 1977, 29.1 years, and 1975, 28.3 years: inmarried male, 1979, 29.6 years, 1977, 29.5 years, and 1975, 27.9 years. For the outmarried female, 1979, 26.6 years; 1977, 26.7 years, and 1975, 24.8 years: the inmarried female, 1979, 26.6 years; 1977, 26.7 years, and 1975, 25.2 years. The mean ages of both brides and grooms do not appear to change appreciably over time.

4. Generation. The generation of the inmarried and outmarried Chinese is shown on Table VI. Generation appears to be one of the most important variables in differentiating between those who marry Chinese and those who prefer non-Chinese spouses. For example in the male population the comparisons between the in and outmarried show the following: 51.2 percent of the outmarried were in the first generation compared to 86.5 percent of the inmarried; 32.6 percent of the outmarried were in the second generation compared to 8.3 percent of the inmarried while 16.3 per-

TABLE III

Chinese Outmarriage by Total and by Sex,
Los Angeles County: 1979, 1977 and 1975

Year	Total Chinese Marriage	Total Outmarriage		Outmarriage by Sex			
		N	%	Male N	%	Female N	%
1979	714	293	41	129	44	164	56
1977	649	322	49.6	141	43.8	181	56.2
1975	596	262	44	99	37.8	163	62.2

TABLE IV

Ethnicity of Non-Chinese Spouse, 1979, 1977 and 1975

Year	Total Outmarriage N	Japanese N	%	Korean N	%	Other* N	%
1979	293	64	21.8	13	4.4	216	73.7
1977	322	56	17.4	8	2.5	258	80.1
1975	262	58	21.1	6	2.3	198	75.6

*Assumed to be white.

TABLE V

Differences Between In and Out Married Chinese by
Age and Sex, in Los Angeles County, 1979

Age	Males (N=550) (Percent) Outmarriage N	%	Inmarriage N	%	Females (N=585) (Percent) Outmarriage N	%	Inmarriage N	%
Under 25	46	35.7	84	20.0	76	46.3	197	46.8
26 - 30	56	43.4	217	51.5	62	37.8	172	40.9
31 - 40	19	14.8	98	23.3	21	12.8	39	9.3
41 - 50	4	3.1	16	3.9	3	1.8	9	2.1
51 & Over	4	3.1	6	1.4	2	1.2	4	1.0

$$x^2 = 16.67* \qquad\qquad\qquad x^2 = 1.86$$

*Statistically significant

cent of the outmarried were in the third generation compared to 5.2 percent of the inmarried. The chi-square of 72.63 is statistically significant.

Similar comparisons were found between the outmarried and inmarried Chinese females. Slightly over fifty percent of the outmarried females were of the first generation compared to 88.4 percent of the inmarried females; 27.4 percent of the outmarried were of the second generation compared to 8.6 precent of the inmarried while 22.0 percent of the outmarried were of the third generation compared to 3.1 percent of the inmarried. The chi-square of 102.17 is statistically significant.

5. *Birthplace of spouse.* A comparison of the birthplace of the spouse between in and outmarried Chinese is shown on Table VII. As birthplace is closely associated

with generation, similar findings between these two variables were found. The highest proportion of both male and female inmarried spouses were China born (75.8 percent and 74.8 percent), while the greatest proportion of the outmarried males and females were born in the United States (48.8 percent for both males and females). The chi-square of 80.59 for males and 99.81 for females is statistically significant.

6. *Number of marriages.* The differences between the in and outmarried Chinese by number of marriages is shown on Table VIII. There is a slight tendency among the outmarried males for less first marriages and more second and third marriages. The chi-square of 6.44 is statistically significant. There is a similar tendency between in and outmarried females but the chi-square of 2.06 is not statistically significant.

TABLE VI

Differences in Generation Between Inmarried and
Outmarried Chinese by Sex, Los Angeles County, 1979

| Generation | I----- M A L E (N=550)---------I | | | | | I-------F E M A L E (N=585)-----I | | | | |
| | | Inmarried | | Outmarried | | | Inmarried | | Outmarried | |
	Total	n	%	n	%	Total	n	%	n	%
1st	430	66	15.3	364	84.7	455	83	18.2	372	81.8
2nd	77	42	54.5	35	45.5	81	45	55.6	36	44.4
3rd	43	21	48.8	22	51.2	49	36	73.5	13	26.5
	550	129		164		585	164		421	

$$x^2 = 72.63* \qquad\qquad x^2 = 102.17*$$

* Statistically significant

TABLE VII

Differences by Birthplace of Spouse Between
Inmarried and Outmarried Chinese by Sex,
Los Angeles County, 1979

| Birthplace | M A L E | | | | | F E M A L E | | | | |
| | | Outmarried | | Inmarried | | | Outmarried | | Inmarried | |
	Total	n	%	n	%	Total	n	%	n	%
China	376	48	13.1	319	86.9	376	61	16.2	315	83.8
Japan	5	2	40.0	3	60.0	4	3	75.0	1	25.0
Korea	5	3	60.0	2	40.0	4	1	25.0	3	45.0
U.S.A.	122	63	51.6	59	48.4	132	80	60.6	52	39.4
Other	51	13	25.5	38	74.5	69	19	27.5	50	72.5
	550	129		421		585	164		421	

TABLE VIII

Differences by Number of Marriages Between
Inmarried and Outmarried Chinese by Sex

Number of Marriage	Number of this Marriage							
	Male				Female			
	Outmarried		Inmarried		Outmarried		Inmarried	
	N	%	N	%	N	%	N	%
1st	112	86.8	380	90.3	149	90.9	398	94.5
2nd	13	10.1	39	9.3	15	9.1	23	5.5
3rd	4	3.1	2	0.5	---	----	---	----
	129	100.0	421	100.1	164	100.0	421	100.0

$$x^2 = 6.44*$$ $$x^2 = 2.06$$

*Statistically significant

7. *Education*. The comparison between the in and outmarried grooms and brides in terms of level of education is shown on Table IX. The inmarried males show a higher proportion in the college graduate and graduate school level than the outmarried males. The outmarried males are higher in the high school and some college level than the inmarried males. The chi-square of 13.99 is statistically significant.

The mean educational level of the inmarried Chinese groom was 16.1 years while the mean educational level of the outmarried Chinese male was 15.4 years. The difference is not statistically significant.

The comparison between the in and outmarried females in education indicates no significant differences between the groups. The chi-square of 1.78 is not statistically significant. The mean educational level of the inmarried Chinese bride was 15.07 years while the mean educational level of the outmarried female was 14.73 years. The difference is not statistically significant.

Although we had similar data for the Chinese for 1979, 1977, and 1975, most of our tables focus on the most recent year. A future paper comparing the Chinese with the Japanese and Korean populations for each of the three years is currently in preparation. For comparative purposes, the Japanese rate of outmarriage for 1979 was 60.6%; for 1977, 63.1%; and 1975, 54.8 percent. The Korean rates were 27.6 percent for 1979; 34.1 percent for 1977 and 26.0 percent for 1975.

Analysis and Discussion

Rates

The most striking finding is the increase in Chinese outmarriage when compared to earlier studies. The rise from under 10 percent in the 1950s to over 40 percent in the 1970s indicates that changes have taken place between the Chinese and other groups in Los Angeles that have lead to the increasing popularity of outmarriages. Variables usually associated with such changes have included: a) internal changes in the ethnic community, most often brought about by culture contact and acculturation which has affected the Chinese family and community and b) external changes, primarily a decrease in the barriers set up by other groups such as prejudice and discrimination.

Internal Changes

Generation and Acculturation

Among the many factors that have contributed to the changes in the rates of out-marriage, generation and acculturation have to be considered among the most important. For example, the first generation immigrant still tends to marry within the group but the second and third generation are not as endogamous. This process is a familiar one, especially for immigrants from Europe so that the term the ''melting pot'' was once considered America's solution to its varied populations. However, the idea that America's non-white groups such as the Asians would or could ever participate in this process was a major question. The barriers of racism, including antimiscegenation laws, were once considered too strong for any significant degree of amalgamation. Therefore it is interesting to note that in a relatively open system for the Chinese in the 1970s the process of integration and racial amalgamation as measured by outmarriage is taking place. Nevertheless it is also interesting to note

Table IX

Differences in Education Between Inmarried and
Outmarried Chinese by Sex, 1979

| Year of Education | Male N=550 | | | | Female N=585 | | | |
| | Outmarried | | Inmarried | | Outmarried | | Inmarried | |
	N	%	N	%	N	%	N	%
Grade School	1	0.8	5	1.2	1	0.6	6	1.4
Some High School	3	2.3	9	2.1	5	3.0	14	3.3
High School	24	18.6	49	11.6	25	15.2	76	18.1
Some College	30	23.3	59	14.0	37	22.6	91	21.6
College Graduate	36	27.9	128	30.4	57	34.8	131	31.1
Graduate School	35	27.1	171	40.6	39	23.8	103	24.5
	129	100.0	421	99.9	164	100.0	421	100.0

$x^2 = 13.99*$ $x^2 = 1.78$
$p = 0.05$ $p = 0.879$

*Statistically significant

that a relatively high proportion of these marriages are not interracial in the strictest sense since they were to Japanese and Koreans.

Generation is most closely related to outmarriage (see Table VI). For example, of the 430 marriages by first generation Chinese males, 15.3 percent were to non-Chinese females; for the first generation Chinese female, 18.2 percent were to non-Chinese grooms. For the second generation male, 54.5 percent were married to non-Chinese while for the female, the outmarriage rate was 55.6 percent. By the third generation, 48.8 percent of the males outmarried while for the third generation Chinese female, of the 49 marriages, 73.5 percent were to non-Chinese grooms. Outmarriage rates are clearly related to generation, with the lowest rates among the first generation Chinese male (15.3 percent) and the highest outmarriage rates by the third generation Chinese female 73.5 percent).

Acculturation

Acculturation adds meaning to generation. Although generation is associated with length of stay in the United States, acculturation introduces the notion of change. For example, a Chinese living in an ethnic ghetto duplicating the life and culture of immigrant parents and surrounded by a hostile white world may survive for several generations with a minimal amount of interaction and change. Acculturation brings about a change in expectations, attitudes, and behavior; modifies and redefines role relationships, affects parental control and power and offers opportunities for out group interaction. This process is familiar—terms such as culture conflict and second generation problems acknowledge some of the difficulties brought about in the transitional process from one culture to another. Although we had no direct measure of acculturation in this study, we assume that the most acculturated group would be the third generation Chinese female who also had the highest outmarriage rates. This position is a product of the loss of parental and family controls, of defining male and female roles in a more modern and liberated fashion, of the small number of available Chinese males, and a desire for a more independent and exciting life style. As one Chinese third generation female told us:

> It would be impossible to even think of marrying a traditional (i.e. old fashioned) Chinese male. He'd want me to stay home and raise a bunch of kids. If I had to marry a Chinese guy, he'd certainly have to have a much more open view of the meaning of a relationship.

It also means economic and housing mobility and opportunities for non-Chinese contacts. A third generation Chinese male said:

> I grew up in an all white suburb. I was about the only Asian in high school so I dated white girls. I still continue to do so and I'll probably get married to one.

Acculturation for the Chinese in the United States has been relatively slow. Lyman (1975) comments that the Chinatowns, whether in San Francisco, New York, Manila, Bangkok, Calcutta, or Liverpool have been remarkably similar in their resistance to integration and the "melting pot." In many countries there has been a resentment concerning the exclusiveness of the Chinese communities, although critics have generally ignored the role of the dominant community in creating the segregated ghettos.

According to Lyman (1974), the major break away from the "Chinatowns" came about during World War II. There was a combination of circumstances such as friendly relations with the Chinese nation; employment opportunities, housing mobility, and the emergence of the American born Chinese American, especially those who were American college educated and of professional status. Many of this new generation opted for better residences outside of Chinatown, although they often reconstituted their community along the lives of the suburban Jews in Chicago (Lyman, 1974:147). This stage reflected cultural pluralism more than full assimilation, and it appears that the children of these Chinese American parents are taking the step toward assimilation and outmarriage.

Outmarriage rates for the Japanese and Korean in Los Angeles County, 1979 also supports the generalization of generation and acculturation. The Japanese rate of outmarriage was 55 percent with the bulk of marriages occurring among the third generation. The Korean rate of outmarriage was 21 percent, with the bulk of inmarriages occurring in the first generation and the highest proportion of the outmarriages taking place in the second and third generation (Kitano and Chai, in press).

Given the power relationships between the ethnic and the dominant society, a certain amount of acculturation, here defined as a movement away from the Chinese towards the American system appears inevitable (Kitano, 1980).

Birthplace

Birthplace and generation are highly correlated, therefore similar relationships were found between place of birth and outmarriage (see Table VII). Of the 367 males born in China, only 13.1 percent married non-Chinese brides, while of the 376 females born in China, 16.2 percent preferred to outmarry. In contrast, of the 122 males born in the United States 51.6 percent chose to outmarry while of the 132 United States born females, 60.6 percent chose non-Chinese husbands.

Previous Marriage

Previous marriages are often related to outmarriage (Golden, 1954; Pavela, 1964; Wirth and Goldhamer, 1944). This variable does not appear important in explaining Chinese outmarriage, primarily because the total number of previous marriages in our population was so small. It may become an important factor if the rates of divorce in the Chinese community rise.

The Family

There are a number of Chinese family typologies that are helpful in understanding marital patterns. Weiss (1977) and Wong (1976) have stratified several types of Chinese families and we have expanded on their categories. We propose the following typologies as related to in and outmarriage.

1. *The traditional family.* By the traditional family we refer to the immigrant families and their views towards outmarriage. We would expect a low rate of outmarriage for these families based on their male, hierarchical structure, the traditional roles of parent and children, problems of language and communication with outsiders, values and life styles.

A 27-year-old, Chinese-born male, when asked about interracial marriage responded, "Definitely not for me. When I want a bowl of Won Ton noodles, she might propose something else. My only choice is a Chinese girl who speaks Cantonese."

2. *The bi-cultural family.* The bi-cultural individual is primarily the second or third generation child from a traditional family, although some first generation immigrants may also adopt this orientation if they had arrived in the United States at a young age. They are products of the exposure to both the Chinese and American cultures and are comfortable with either Chinese or American acquaintances. Although there may be instances of culture conflict and marginality, there are also many examples of the successful integration of the cultures. Marriages for this group will be based more on opportunity, housing location, and the choice of schools since the individual will not deliberately set out to look for a spouse of a specific ethnicity.

A 30-year-old inmarried first generation Chinese lady provides a picture of this category. She is quite westernized in appearance and in her thinking; she drives a sports car, wears designer jeans but prefers Chinese food. She has friends in both cultures and considers herself bi-cultural. She has no negative attitudes towards people who outmarry but had not personally considered marrying out of the Chinese group herself.

3. *The modern family.* Weiss (1977) describes the modernists as cosmopolitan, middle class, and more typically American than Chinese. They desire full acculturation to American ways and even their ethnic organizations reflect American, rather than Chinese models. At the extreme, they would speak, think, and write "American" and the only reminder of a Chinese heritage would be their physical features. We would expect a high outmarriage rate from this group. As one Chinese lady told us, "I would not exclude the idea of eventually marrying a Chinese man but I prefer going out with someone more attractive. You know in public places I would feel more comfortable with someone who is more Americanized than me—the more American the more I feel accepted."

There are also other marital patterns. One pattern, most common in the 1950s and 1960s was the older, single male turning to Hong Kong for wives. These "American uncles," a pejorative term referring to the often dull, inexpressive middle-aged Chinese male from the United States were a product of the early skewed immigration pattern, discrimination, the ghettoization of the Chinese, and the lack of available women in America. There are also currently younger Chinese males who have found difficulty in getting acquainted with the more acculturated Chinese American female turning to Hong Kong or Taiwan for their brides. It is still rare for females to search for grooms in the old country.

There were also several other types of families. Lai (1980:223) mentions the "slot system" which took place when Chinese immigration was banned. The immigrant Chinese male would return to China and duly report the birth of a child, even if such a birth did not actually take place, to the proper authorities, thereby creating a slot, or papers for immigration. These children were often referred to as "paper sons" and the slots could be sold to the highest bidder.

Sung (1967:155) describes another type of Chinese family. She refers to the "mutilated family," a family united in a marital bond, but separated physically. The Chinese male would be in the United States while the family were in China, which explains why there were four times as many married Chinese men as married Chinese women in the 1930 U.S. Census. According to Sung, the mutilated marriage was the predominant form of family life among Chinese men until the passage of more liberal immigration legislation in 1943.

Finally, Wong (1976) mentions some often ignored groups such as sailors who have jumped ship and illegal aliens who live on marginal incomes. Very little data are available on these populations, although it would be reasonable to assume that they would inmarry if they ever married at all.

External Changes

Anti-miscegenation laws were in effect in California from 1850 to 1948. Although prejudice, discrimination, and segregation still exists, there is little question that opportunities in education, in housing, and in social interaction have improved over the past several decades. Upward mobility, increasing acceptance, and equal status contact are correlated with interracial marriage.

It should be noted that the Asian female seems generally more accepted (and acceptable) to the dominant group. For example in Los Angeles, two of the major networks employ Asian anchorwomen in their news programs (one Chinese American, one Japanese American) and a similar pattern is seen in San Francisco and Honolulu. Asian males, if portrayed at all, play the role of houseservant and cook. Although the peaceful image can be viewed as an improvement over the gooks and communist fanatics seen during World War II, the Korean War and the hostilities in Vietnam (Iiyama and Kitano, in press), the neutered Chinese male stereotype may be one factor in the lower male rates of outermarriage.

There are a number of other factors related to marriage. Attractiveness, sexuality, and the idea of "falling in love" remain as powerful explanations for people getting together. We acknowledge the importance of these factors, as well as the importance of arranged marriages, but had no access to this kind of information. There is also the popularity of people living together and there are no doubt many interracial couples who do, but again, there are little available data.

Finally, the topic of interracial marriage is a value question and can invoke a variety of feelings. For some it may be viewed as the very essence of American democracy so that any rise in the rates is cause for jubilation, while for others, it may be viewed as a symptom of moral decay and the breakdown and bastardization of the American system.

BIBLIOGRAPHY

Barnett, Larry D. "Interracial Marriage in California." *Marriage and Family Living*. Nov. 1963, *25*, 425–427.

Burma, John. "Interethnic Marriage in Los Angeles, 1948–1959." *Social Forces*, 1963, *42*, 156–165.

Char, Walter, Wen-sheng, Tseng, Kwong-yen Lum and Jing Hsu. "The Chinese," *People and Cultures of Hawaii*. Edited by John McDermott, Wen-sheng Tseng and Thomas Marezki. Honolulu: University of Hawaii Press, 1980, 53–72.

Golden, J. "Patterns of Negro-White Intermarriage." *Social Forces*. March 1954, *36*, 267–269.

Iiyama, Patricia and Harry H.L. Kitano. "Asian Americans in the Media." 1981 (Manuscript in process).

Kitano, Harry H.L. *Race Relations*. (Revised Edition). Englewood Cliffs, NJ: Prentice-Hall, 1980.

Kitano, Harry H.L., and Lynn Chai. "Korean Interracial Marriage," 1981 (in press).

Lai, H.M. "Chinese," *Harvard Encyclopedia of American Ethnic Groups*. Edited by S. Thernstorm, A. Orlov and O. Handlin. Cambridge: Harvard University Press, 1980, 217–234.

Lyman, Standord. *Chinese Americans*. New York: Random House, 1974.

Lyman, Stanford. "Contrasts in the Community Organization of Chinese and Japanese in America." *Majority and Minority*. Edited by Norman Yetman and C. Hoy Steele. Boston: Allyn and Bacon, 2nd Edition, 1975, 285–296.

Pavela, T.H. "An Exploratory Study of Negro-White Intermarriage in Indiana." *Marriage and Family Living*. May 1964, *26*(2), 209–211.

Risdon, Randall. "A Study of Interracial Marriages Based on Data for Los Angeles County," *Sociology and Social Research*, 1954, *39*, 92–95.

Sung, Betty Lee. *Mountain of Gold*. New York: McMillan, 1967.

Weiss, Melford. "The Research Experience in a Chinese-American Community," *Journal of Social Issues*, 1977, *33*(4), 120–132.

Wirth, L. and H. Goldenhamer. "The Hybrid and the Problem of Miscegenation." *Characteristics of the American Negro*. Edited by O. Klineberg. New York: Harper and Row, 1944, 249–369.

Wong, Bernard. "Social Stratification, Adaptive Strategies, and the Chinese Community of New York." *Urban Life*, April 1976, *5*(1), 33–52.

INTERETHNIC MARRIAGE AND DIVORCE IN HAWAII: A PANEL STUDY OF 1968 FIRST MARRIAGES

Margaret M. Schwertfeger

Despite considerable variation in the forms and functions of marriage across time and space, marriages are meant to endure. This goal of marital stability seems to underlie the principle of endogamy or the mandate to marry one's kind. The meaning of "one's kind" as well as the basis for legitimizing only certain mates as marriage candidates, varies in both traditional and contemporary societies.

Social scientists and clinicians have addressed the principles underlying mate selection (Winch, 1958; Parkman and Sawyer, 1967; Leon, 1975; Maretzki, 1977) and the effects of interethnic choices on marital outcome (Adams, 1937; Lind, 1964; Carter and Click, 1970; Sanborn, 1977; and Monahan, 1979). While these two issues are clearly related, this article addresses the latter. More specifically, are interethnic marriages in Hawaii more likely to end in divorce than are homogamous marriages? Do the costs which anecdotal evidence suggests are associated with interethnic marriages (i.e., communication barriers, social isolation, familial rejection) make these marriages especially vulnerable to divorce? Do members of ethnic groups showing a high incidence of interethnic marriage also demonstrate high divorce rates regardless of whom they marry? Are interethnic marriages more stable in environments such as Hawaii where they are more common? Finally, do previous research findings on interethnic marriage and divorce obtain when quasi-longitudinal data are employed?

Hawaii's Unique Ethnic Composition

Hawaii's rich history involving relatively large scale migrations from countries with both eastern and western traditions has earned it the reputation as the melting pot of the Pacific. Members of diverse ethnic groups not only interact freely, they also intermarry.

By 1979, close to 30% of the estimated 800,000 civilian residents of Hawaii specified their ethnic background as mixed; two-thirds of these were part-Hawaiian. At present, three ethnic groups account for close to 70% of the population: Japanese (27%), Hawaiians and Part-Hawaiians (22%), and Caucasians and Portuguese (21%).

Margaret M. Schwertfeger is a Research Analyst, State Department of Health, Hawaii.

49

Other groups include Filipinos (11%), Mixed non-Hawaiian (10%), Chinese (5%), Korean (2%), Samoan (1.5%), and Puerto Rican, Blacks, and others (1.5%).

Because Hawaii's ethnic complexion is ideally suited for investigation into the relationships between ethnic intermarriage and marital outcome, numerous previous studies have been conducted.

Romanzo Adams (1937) concluded, based on his analysis of Hawaii's marriage and divorce records prior to 1935, that ethnic groups which are the most disorganized (i.e., "with the least effective control over their members," P. 225) have the highest rates of interracial marriage and the highest rates of divorce. However, the divorce rates within these groups are approximately equal when comparing the in-married with the outmarried categories.

Although subsequent researchers have found it difficult to operationalize the concept of social disorganization used by Adams in 1937, one of Adams' students, Andrew Lind, tested Adams' hypotheses utilizing interethnic marriage and divorce data from 1956 through 1962. He found that, in fact, the two groups with highest inter-marriage rates (Hawaiians and Koreans) also demonstrated highest divorce rates while the Japanese, with the lowest incidence of interethnic marriage, showed the lowest divorce rates. However, no clear pattern emerged for the other ethnic groups under study (Chinese, Filipinos, Puerto Ricans, Caucasians, and Blacks). In fact, the Chinese showed a dramatic increase in the rate of out-marriage but maintained a remarkably low divorce rate, second only to the Japanese. Lind also noted that Hawaiians, Koreans, Puerto Ricans, Filipinos, and Caucasians lowered the probability of divorce if they intermarried with members of more highly organized groups.

Lind (1964) concluded that from the perspective of the oriental partner (Chinese or Japanese) marrying interethnically increases the probability of marital breakdown, while from the perspective of the non-oriental, intermarriage to an oriental lowered the likelihood of divorce, with the exception that the Caucasian wife marrying a Japanese or Chinese male increased the probability of divorce.

This finding on the intraction effect between the sex and ethnicities of the marital partners was consistent with that reported previously by Cheng and Yamamura (1957) and subsequently by Hanabusa (1974). With the exception of Hanabusa (1974) who looked at a 1968 marriages cohort over a five-year period, methodological problems haunt the results of previous research.

All previous researchers based their conclusions on the ratio of the number of divorces to marriages in the same or adjacent years. Also, as the divorces included both first and subsequent marriages, persons employed by the military, and marriages of both non-residents and residents, the results may have been affected by shifts in migration patterns and persons contracting multiple marriages.

With the computerization of information on the marriage and divorce certificates it is now feasible to control for outside sources of variation by following a cohort of first marriages over time. This longitudinal panel design, therefore, represents an improvement over other methods used previously.

Study Design and Method

In order to establish the validity of previous cross-sectional findings in the relationship between ethnicity, interethnic marriage, and divorce, Hawaii civilian residents were observed at the time of their first marriage (as reported on their marriage certificate in 1968) and again, at the time of their divorce if it occurred in Hawaii within nine years or less. The results below do not include marriages which were terminated by the death of a spouse, separation (formal or informal), or those for which divorce papers were filed but never completed. Marriages terminated outside Hawaii were also necessarily omitted.

In order to maximize the probability that the couples in the 1968 marriage cohort would have remained in Hawaii during this time period and would have been "at risk" to divorce here, all non-residents and military personnel were dropped from the analysis.

The following results are based on 3,405 first marriages of Hawaii residents recorded in 1968. By the end of September, 1976, approximately 16% (or 544) of these marriages had been terminated in Hawaii.

As shown in Table 1, the ethnic heritage of the individuals in the 1968 marriage cohort parallels that of the 1968 general population. However, differences in the coding schemas preclude an in-depth analysis of variations.

Interethnic Marriages

Table 2 reports the rates of interethnic marriages for brides and grooms in 1968. Approximately 41% of all the marriages were interethnic with highest rates seen for Chinese brides (69%) and grooms (67%) followed by persons in especially small groups represented in the "other" category (60% brides; 66% grooms).

Close to half of the Hawaiian and Part-Hawaiian marriages (49% brides and grooms) and those of Caucasians and Portuguese (48% brides; 47% grooms) were interethnic. Japanese brides (24%) and grooms (21%) showed the lowest incidence of interethnic marriages. This finding is consistent with Adams (1937) Cheng and Yamamura (1957), Lind (1964), Glick (1970), Hanabusa (1974). These data and those reported by Glick (1970) suggest an apparent trend toward increased outmarriage among Japanese in Hawaii, although intermarriage rates are still the lowest of all ethnic groups in Hawaii.

Tables 3 and 4 show the sex-ethnic combinations in the marriage cohort under study. As predicted by Parkman and Sawyer (1964) and Leon (1975) members of ethnic groups out-marry most frequently with members of ethnic groups with similar cultural traditions. Chinese and Japanese who out-marry are most inclined to marry each other. Hawaiian and Part-Hawaiian brides and grooms who out-marry are most inclined to marry Caucasians, Portuguese or Filipinos.

The results of the panel study shown in Table 5 indicate that a lower proportion

Table 1

Ethnic Composition of Hawaii's 1968 Civilian Population
and First Marriage Cohort Under Study (1968)

Ethnic Group[1]	(Est.) 1968 Civilian Population[2]	1968 First Marriage Cohort (Hawaii Residents Only)
All groups	100% (665,900)	100% (6,810)
Caucasian	19.0%	19.6%
Japanese	34.3%	33.9%
Chinese	6.2%	5.6%
Filipino	8.8%	12.8%
Hawaiian & Part Hawaiian	21.0%	22.1%
Mixed (Non-Hawaiian)	9.8%	(not available)
Other includes	.9%	6.1%
Korean	N/A	(1.3%)
Black	N/A	(.3%)
Puerto Rican	(in Caucasian)	(1.6%)
Samoan	N/A	(2.0%)
Other or unknown	N/A	(.9%)

[1] The Caucasian category includes Portugese and others of European extraction, and the "other" category includes Koreans, Blacks, Puerto Ricans, Samoans and persons listed as "other" or unknown on the 1968 marriage certificate. These categories hold throughout this study.

[2] Source: State of Hawaii Data Book (1969, p. 13). Excludes armed services personnel and dependents, persons in institutions, on Niihau or in Kalawao County.

of the marriages of Chinese (13%) and Japanese (14%) end in early divorce than for Filipinos (18%), Caucasians, and Portuguese (18%) and Part-Hawaiians (19%). These results are consistent with previous findings except that the differences are slight.

Inter-Intra Ethnic Differences

Table 6 shows the early divorce rates for same and interethnic marriages for males and females of each of the five major ethnic groups. Overall, interethnic marriages are more likely to end in divorce (19.2% compared to 13.8%). This pattern holds for everyone except that Hawaiian and Part-Hawaiian women and Caucasian and Portuguese men do not increase their likelihood of divorce by marrying outside their respective ethnic groups. No intramarriages involving Chinese ended in divorce within nine years but when they inter-married their divorce rates approached those for other groups marrying within their own ethnic groups. Divorce rates of Filipinos doubled when they married interethnically (from 11 to 21% for women and 11 to 23% for men). These results are consistent with previous findings, although again, the differences are less than reported earlier.

Results for Particular Sex-Ethnic Combinations

Table 7 presents early divorce rates by the particular sex-ethnic combination. Caucasian and Portuguese women show the lowest divorce rate if they marry Japanese males (13.2%) while Caucasian and Portuguese males divorce least within nine years when they marry Chinese women (7.4%). Caucasian, Portuguese, and Filipino combinations appear to be at most risk to divorce for both brides and grooms (22.9% for Caucasian and Portuguese grooms who marry Filipinos and 24.1% for Caucasian and Portuguese brides marrying Filipinos). Hawaiian and Part-Hawaiian women appear especially prone to divorce if they marry Chinese or Filipinos, while Hawaiian and Part-Hawaiian males show highest divorce rates when they marry Chinese women (25.0%), women of "Other" ethnicities (22.9%) and Caucasian and Portuguese women (21.3%). Except for those who marry Hawaiian and Part-Hawaiian males (25.0%) Chinese women show especially low divorce rates no matter whom they marry, while Chinese males appear most likely to divorce when they marry non-oriental women (14.5%). Filipino brides indicate a higher probability of divorce unless they marry other Filipinos or Hawaiian and Part-Hawaiian males. In fact, the divorce

Table 2

Percent of First Marriages Which were Interethnic
by Ethnic Group and Sex
Hawaii 1968-76 Panel Data

Ethnic Group	Women	Men
Total (1392/3402)	41%	41%
Caucasian	48.3%	47.2%
Hawaiian & Part Hawaiian	48.5%	49.2%
Chinese	68.9%	66.8%
Filipino	41.6%	45.3%
Japanese	23.9%	20.7%
Other	60.3%	66.3%

Table 3

Intra and Interethnic First Marriages per 1,000 Brides
by Ethnicity of Bride and Groom
Hawaii, 1968-76 Panel Study
N = 3402 Marriages

Bride's Ethnicity	Groom's Ethnicity							Total Percent[1]	Total Marriages
	Caucasian	Hawaiian & Part Haw'n	Chinese	Filipino	Japanese	Other	Unknown		
Caucasian	517	230	36	86	79	52	[1]	100%	[673]
Hawaiian & Part Haw'n	177	515	20	121	94	72	[1]	99.9%	[745]
Chinese	138	163	311	41	296	51		100%	[196]
Filipino	114	159	26	584	69	48		100%	[421]
Japanese	56	70	59	30	761	25		100.1%	[1178]
Other	201	185	21	69	127	397	[1]	100%	[189]

[1] The ethnicity of three of the grooms under study was unavailable. These marriages were therefore dropped from the percentages. The percentages may not add to 100% due to rounding error.

Table 4

Intra and Interethnic First Marriages per 1,000 Grooms
by Ethnicity of Bride and Groom
Hawaii, 1968-76 Panel Study
N = 3402 Marriages

Groom's Ethnicity	Bride's Ethnicity						Total Percent[1]	Total Marriages
	Caucasian	Hawaiian & Part Haw'n	Chinese	Filipino	Japanese	Other		
Caucasian	528	200	41	73	100	58	100%	[659]
Hawaiian & Part Haw'n	205	508	42	89	110	46	100%	[756]
Chinese	130	82	332	60	375	22	100.1%	[184]
Filipino	129	200	18	547	78	29	100.1%	450
Japanese	47	62	51	26	793	21	100%	1130
Other	157	242	45	90	130	337	100.1%	223
Unknown	[1]	[1]				[1]		[3]

[1] The ethnicity of three of the grooms under study was unavailable. These cases were therefore dropped from the percentages. The percentages may not add to 100% due to rounding error.

Table 5

Percent of First Marriages Ending in Divorce by Ethnicity
Hawaii, 1968-76 Panel Study

Ethnicity[1]	Percent
Chinese	13.2 [42/319]
Japanese	14.0 [198/1412]
Filipino	17.6 [110/625]
Caucasian	17.8 [175/984]
Hawaiian & Part Hawaiian	19.3 [216/1117]
Other	20.8 [70/337]

[1] Includes all marriages in which at least one spouse is a member of the designated ethnic group.

Table 6

Percent of Marriages Ending in Divorce Within Nine Years
for Intra and Interethnic Marriages of Brides and Grooms[1]
Hawaii, 1968-76 Panel Study

Bride's Ethnicity	Intra-Ethnic	Inter-Ethnic	Groom's Ethnicity	Intra-Ethnic	Inter-Ethnic
Chinese	-0- [0]	14.1 [19]	Chinese	-0- [0]	18.7 [23]
Japanese	12.2 [109]	18.8 [53]	Japanese	12.2 [109]	15.4 [36]
Filipino	11.0 [27]	20.6 [36]	Filipino	11.0 [27]	23.4 [47]
Caucasian	16.4 [57]	20.9 [68]	Caucasian	16.4 [57]	16.1 [50]
Hawaiian and Part Hawaiian	19.3 [74]	18.6 [67]	Hawaiian and Part Hawaiian	19.3 [74]	20.2 [75]
Other	13.3 [10]	21.1 [24]	Other	13.2 [10]	24.3 [36]
Total	13.8 [277]	19.2 [267]	Total	13.8 [277]	19.2 [267]

[1] The numbers in parentheses in each cell refer to the number of divorces while the percentage refers to the number of divorces/number of marriages. For the number of marriages see the previous Table 2.

Table 7

Percent of Marriages Ending in Divorce Within Nine Years
by Ethnicity of Bride and Groom
Hawaii, 1968-76 Panel Study

Bride's Ethnicity	Groom's Ethnicity						Total
	Chinese	Filipino	Japanese	Caucasian	Hawaiian & Part Haw'n	Other	
Chinese	0 [0]	12.5 [1]	10.3 [6]	7.4 [2]	25.0 [8]	20.0 [2]	9.7 [19]
Japanese	14.5 [10]	20.0 [7]	12.2 [109]	15.2 [10]	19.3 [16]	34.5 [10]	13.8 [162]
Filipino	27.3 [3]	11.0 [27]	20.7 [6]	22.9 [11]	14.9 [10]	30.0 [6]	15.0 [63]
Caucasian	20.8 [5]	24.1 [14]	13.2 [7]	16.4 [57]	21.3 [33]	25.7 [9]	18.6 [125]
Hawaiian & Part Haw'n	26.7 [4]	24.4 [22]	17.1 [12]	15.2 [20]	19.3 [74]	16.7 [9]	18.9 [141]
Other	25.0 [1]	3.1 [3]	20.8 [5]	18.4 [7]	22.9 [8]	13.3 [10]	18.0 [34]
Total	12.5 [23]	16.4 [74]	12.8 [145]	16.2 [107]	19.7 [149]	20.6 [46]	16.0 [544]

rate for Filipino brides and Hawaiian and Part-Hawaiian males is lower than that for two Hawaiians (14.9% and 19.3% respectively). Apparently, the marriages of Filipino grooms are most stable when they marry Filipino and Chinese brides (11.0% and 12.5%) as 20% or more of their marriages to women of other ethnic groups end in divorce within nine years. Marriages of Japanese brides to Chinese, and Caucasian and Portuguese males are respectively stable (14.5% and 15.2% respectively). Similar patterns hold for Japanese males married to Caucasian and Portuguese and Chinese females (13.2% and 10.3% respectively). However, approximately 20% of the marriages of Japanese males and females to Filipinos end in divorce within nine years.

Conclusions

In sum, the findings based on a longitudinal panel design support the previously reported slightly lower divorce rates for Japanese and Chinese males and females. These data also underscore the remarkable stability of Chinese in-marriages in comparison to those of all other ethnic groups. Not a single marriage between two persons of Chinese ancestry ended in divorce in Hawaii within approximately nine years. This finding certainly suggests further investigation into the norms and familial organization of this ethnic group.

While the overall divorce rate is higher for interethnic than for same ethnic marriages, previously reported interaction effects between the sex and ethnicities of the partners persist. Caucasian and Portuguese males show the lowest divorce rates when they marry Chinese and Japanese females. However, the pattern does not hold for Caucasian and Portuguese women marrying Chinese males.

The absence of easily recognizable patterns showing a relationship between interethnic marriage and divorce suggests that perhaps where interethnic marriage is relatively common, a person's ethnicity may be less relevant in both mate selection and marital success. Clearly, other factors must be considered before any firm conclusions can be drawn from data demonstrating rather weak percentage point differences in the divorce rates of marriages composed of various sex-ethnic combinations.

REFERENCES

Adams, Romanzo. *Interracial Marriage in Hawaii*. New York: MacMillan Press, 1937, 205–226.
Carter, Hugh and P. C. Click. *Marriage and Divorce: a Social and Economic Study*. Cambridge: Harvard University Press, 1970.
Cheng, C. K., and D. Yamamura. "Interracial marriage and divorce in Hawaii." *Social Forces*, 1957, *36*: 77–84.
Glick, Clarence C. "Interracial Marriage and Admixture in Hawaii." *Social Biology*, 1970, *17*: 278–291.
Hanabusa, Colleen. "Interethnic Marriage and Divorce in Hawaii." (Unpublished Paper.) Department of Sociology, University of Hawaii, 1974.

Leon, Joseph J. "Sex-ethnic marriage in Hawaii: a nonmetric multidimensional analysis." *Journal of Marriage and the Family* Nov. 1975: 775–781.

Lind, Andrew. "Interracial marriage as affecting divorce in Hawaii." *Sociology and Social Research*, 1964, *49*: 17–26.

Maretzki, Thomas. "Intercultural marriage: an introduction," in Tseng, McDermott, and Maretzki (eds.), *Adjustment in Intercultural Marriage*. Honolulu: University Press of Hawaii, 1977, 1–11.

Monahan, Thomas P. "Interracial marriage and divorce in Kansas and the question of instability of mixed marriages," in G. Kurian (ed.), *Cross-cultural Perspectives in Mate Selection and Marriage*. Westport, CT: Greenwood Press, 1979, 350–363.

Parkman, Margaret A. and J. Sawyer. "Dimensions of Interethnic Marriage in Hawaii." *American Sociological Reivew*, 1967, *32*: 593–607.

Sanborn, Kenneth. "Intercultural Marriage in Hawaii," in Tseng, McDermott, and Maretzki (eds.), *Adjustment in Intercultural Marriage*. Honolulu: University Press of Hawaii, 1977, 41–50.

Winch, Robert. *Mate Selection*. New York: Harper Brothers, 1958.

INTERMARRIAGE AND ASSIMILATION
IN A PLURAL SOCIETY:
JAPANESE-AMERICANS IN THE UNITED STATES

John N. Tinker

Racial intermarriage is a sensitive and emotion-charged issue in the United States. While, in the last twenty years, people have increasingly come to agree that public facilities ought to be desegregated and that members of all races ought to have equal opportunities for jobs, many people remain skeptical or even hostile about racial intermarriage (Greeley and Sheatsley, 1974). For example, a 1972 poll of national opinion showed that 60% of the respondents at that time disapproved of marriage between whites and nonwhites (Gallup, 1978).

It is because intermarriage is such a sensitive issue that it is interesting to those of us who are concerned about the course of race relations in this country. As the long history of social distance research has shown, normative prohibitions against intermarriage form the last boundary between groups (Ehrlich, 1973). Milton Gordon's influential model of the assimilation process also recognizes that widespread intermarriage is the final step in the assimilation of a minority group. After the old country ways have been adapted to fit in with the new culture (cultural assimilation), after business associations and friendships are formed between members of the immigrant group, or their children, and members of the dominant society (structural assimilation), the final step is marital assimilation (Gordon, 1964). Intermarriage rates and patterns, then, can tell us a good deal about the state of the separation between groups; is it a chasm that nobody crosses or are there bridges that span the gulf and networks of relations that are starting to knit the groups into one whole? Robert Merton (1941) in his seminal paper on intermarriage, indicated why this is such a productive issue for students of race relations. He pointed out that the norms of social distance and deference that keep minority groups apart from the dominant society in which they are embedded are directly challenged by the norms of intimacy and social accessibility which govern the family. When the gulf between groups is great and intermarriages are few, the network of intimate ties in an extended family may be torn apart by a marriage which crosses a group boundary. When the intermarriage rate is high, however, this both suggests that the norm of distance between

John N. Tinker, Ph.D., is affiliated with the Department of Sociology, California State University, Fresno.

the groups has lost its force and signals the knitting together of the groups by an intricate web of intimate family ties. It is for this reason that Japanese intermarriage in the United States is interesting to students of minority relations. By studying the rates and patterns of intermarriage, we can learn about the current place of the Japanese minority and, more important, we can learn something about the importance of race itself in this society.

The United States has been characterized as a racist society, a society in which the color of a person's skin has more to do with his life-chances than the qualities of his mind or the diligence of his efforts. For example, Robert Blauner, describing the United States as a colonial society, writes: "The final component of colonization is racism. Racism is a principle of social domination by which a group seen as inferior or different in alleged biological characteristics is exploited, controlled, and oppressed socially and psychically by a superordinate group" (1972:84). It is undeniable that the United States has been a racist society. The history of Japanese settlement on the West Coast illustrates this clearly. The first generation of Japanese immigrants were denied the chance to become naturalized citizens. In addition, in California, there were restrictions against their ownership of land. Also, during World War II, Japanese-Americans on the West Coast, citizens and aliens alike, were forcibly detained in "relocation centers." Finally, in many states, there were laws preventing intermarriage with whites. A law of this sort was in force in California, for example, until 1948 (Simpson and Yinger, 1958:553).

It is undeniable that the United States has been a racist society; the important question, now, is whether the racism in this society is ineradicable. It is here that studying Japanese-American intermarriage can be especially instructive. The Japanese-Americans are a racially distinct group in a society in which racial distinctions are thought to have enormous importance. Unlike an Italian-American or a Polish-American, a Japanese-American wears his ethnic identity on his face. He cannot, by changing his name or changing his accent, fade into the "American" crowd. Whatever he does, he still looks Oriental. How important is this racial boundary now? Has it, as the early supporters of a restrictive immigration policy argued, made the Japanese an unassimilable minority in the United States (Simpson and Yinger, 1972:118)? Or, in the case of the Japanese in America, is it losing its force? Are the Japanese-Americans assimilating in spite of their racial distinctiveness? By examining Japanese-American intermarriage, we can measure the assimilation of the Japanese and we can, at the same time, assess the importance of race as a social boundary in this society. In this paper, I will survey the available research on Japanese-American intermarriage in order to determine the rate of that intermarriage, the patterns that it has followed, and, most important, what this tells us about the assimilation of a racially distinct, at one time systematically oppressed, minority group in this society.

Rates of Intermarriage

Table 1 summarizes the rate of intermarriage in the continental U.S. shown in a number of studies now available. The data are organized by decade, from the 1940s to the present. The first thing to look at is the most recent data. Three studies

TABLE 1

JAPANESE INTERMARRIAGES IN CONTINENTAL U.S.,
BY DECADE AND REGION

	Number of Marriages Involving Japanese Partners	Number of Intermarriages	%
1940-49			
United States, 1940-49[1]	29,202	4,362	14.9%
Los Angeles, 1949[2]	187	20	10.7%
1950-59			
U.S., 1950-59[1]	32,982	17,500	53.1%
California, 1955-59[2]	4,168	1,030	24.7%
Los Angeles, 1950-59[2]	2,935	576	19.6%
1960-69			
U.S., 1960-69[1]	34,208	18,239	53.3%
Los Angeles, 1960-61[3]	508	345	67.9%
Fresno, CA, 1960-69[4]	263	79	30%
Sacramento, CA, 1961-70[5]	-	-	28.3%
1970-			
Los Angeles, 1971-72[2]	1,160	551	47.5%
Fresno, CA, 1970-71[4]	85	41	48.2%
San Francisco, CA, 1971[6]	-	-	58.0%

1. U.S. Bureau of the Census: 1970, Table 12
2. Kikumura and Kitano:1973, Table 1 and Table 2
3. Burma et al.:1970, Table 1
4. Tinker: 1973, Table 1
5. Conner: 1974
6. Omatsu: 1972

(Kikumura and Kitano, Omatsu, Tinker) report intermarriage rates for the early 1970s. These local studies (they were done in Los Angeles, San Francisco, and Fresno, California) are the most recent that have been published and they are consistent in what they show. In each of those areas, the intermarriage rate is around 50 percent. That is, about 50 percent of the marriages with at least one Japanese partner were intermarriages in those three California cities.

This high rate of intermarriage is, in general, consistent with the data available for the previous decade. For this period, the decade of the 1960s, there are four data sources available. Three of these, again, are local studies, reporting intermarriage rates in California cities (Burma et al., Conner, Tinker), while the fourth is the 5-percent sample of the 1970 Census of Population. For this period, the local studies are more variable than are those reporting 1970s data. The two studies done in in- land California cities, Fresno and Sacramento, report intermarriage rates of about 30 percent. The Los Angeles study, on the other hand, reports an intermarriage rate of nearly 70 percent. The Census found that 53.3 percent of all the marriages with at least one Japanese partner which were initiated in the 1960s and survived until the census day in 1969 were intermarriages. While there is some variability in these studies, the data on the intermarriage of people of Japanese descent in the United States in the 1960s and the beginning of the 1970s strongly support an important conclusion: i.e., race has not formed an impenetrable boundary sealing them off from the rest of the society. The United States has, with reason, been called a racist society and the discrimination against Japanese in this country was systematic and severe through World War II. The data on intermarriage indicate a very high rate of marital assimilation now, however, suggesting that the racial boundary which was once thought so important that it was used to justify major national policies, such as immigration laws and the whole process of relocation, has almost faded away.

Hawaii

Hawaii is generally treated separately from the rest of the United States when rates and patterns of intermarriage are considered. This is because Hawaii is unique in several respects. In the first place, people in Hawaii have long been thought to have a set of values accepting or even supporting racial intermarriage rather than the values disapproving it which have been common on the mainland (Adams, 1937; Glick, 1970). There has also been a demographic substructure supporting those values which has distinguished Hawaii from the mainland states. That is, large and influential groups of settlers, the Caucasians among them, had, for a long time in Hawaii, radically imbalanced sex ratios (Cheng and Yamamura, 1957; Glick, 1970). They typically had more males than females and this imbalance encouraged intermarriage as the excess males sought wives outside their own groups. Hawaii is unique in the United States also in having a non-white (chiefly Pacific and Asian) majority. The imbalanced sex ratios which characterized several of the immigrant groups in Hawaii and the special values of the islands have led to a very high rate of intermarriage so that Hawaii has often been seen as America's Pacific melting pot.

The Japanese, on the other hand, have been thought to be a peculiar case in Hawaii, with a relatively low rate of intermarriage when compared with other island groups (Adams, 1937; Cheng and Yamamura, 1957). Adams, for example, wrote: "they marry within their own group in higher proportion than any other of the peoples of Hawaii" (1937:160). This was explained by the relatively large size of the Japanese population in Hawaii and the even sex ratio within it. Both of these factors made it possible for Japanese grooms to find Japanese brides and vice versa. In addition, it was argued that the Japanese had especially strong group and family controls over marriage; controls which, by limiting intermarriage, limited assimilation. The most recent data, reported in Table 2, indicate that, while the Japanese had a relatively low rate of intermarriage (for Hawaii) through the 1950s, their intermarriage rate has recently increased substantially. In fact, Kikumura and Kitano report that 47 percent of all the marriages of Japanese in Hawaii in 1970 were intermarriages. That rate is quite comparable with recent rates found in local studies on the mainland; it suggests that in Hawaii, as in the continental United States, the racial boundary is being bridged by intermarriage.

TABLE 2

JAPANESE INTERMARRIAGES IN HAWAII

	Number of Marriages Involving Japanese Partners	Number of Intermarriages	%
1920-30[1]	8,521	480	5.6%
1930-40	10,766	1,086	10.1%
1940-49	17,539	3,489	19.9%
1950-59	18,849	4,691	24.9%
1960-69	17,537	6,796	38.8%
1960-69[2]	14,070	4,036	28.7%
1965-69[3]	9,558	4,046	42%
1970[4]	2,350	1,107	47%

1. Glick, C.:1970, Recalculated from Table 1
2. U.S. Bureau of the Census:1970, Table 13
3. Leon:1975
4. Kikumura & Kitano:1973, Table 3

Patterns of Intermarriage

The studies which we have reviewed so far clearly indicate that the rate of Japanese intermarriage in the United States is quite high. We should next examine the patterns in those marriages. That is, do the studies show some pattern of changes in rates over time, or patterns in the sorts of people who intermarry? Any regularities of this sort that we can find will help us to interpret the rates that we looked at, above, and will help us to understand the impact of these rates on the groups involved.

Generations: Issei, Nisei, Sansei

The first pattern that appears in those studies which have detailed enough information to show it, is that the rate of intermarriage is much greater for the Sansei (the second generation of Japanese born in this country) than it was for the Nisei (the children of Japanese immigrants). Eric Woodrum (1978), for example, analyzed data collected by the Japanese-American Research Project at the University of California at Los Angeles. These data are drawn from a large sample of Issei (immigrants) in the continental United States whose names were on the membership lists of various Japanese associations, their children (the Nisei) and their grandchildren (the Sansei). This sampling design probably over-represents whose families are involved in Japanese-American association activities and correspondingly underrepresents those who are more peripheral to these organizations and, perhaps, better assimilated (see Montero and Tsukashima, 1977, for a discussion of this problem). These data may, therefore, underreport the total intermarriage rate but they do allow us, within the same set of families, to compare the experiences of Nisei and Sansei. The difference is striking. The Nisei members of these families have an intermarriage rate of about 10 percent while their children, the Sansei, were intermarrying at a 37 percent rate by 1967 (Woodrum, 1978:85–85). The data from Fresno, California (Tinker, 1973) show an equally dramatic relationship between generation and intermarriage rate. Between 1958 and 1971, 17 percent of the marriages with at least one Nisei partner in Fresno County were intermarriages while 58 percent of the marriages involving only Japanese-Americans whose parents were born in the United States (Sansei) were intermarriages.

This pattern of increasing intermarriage by generation shows up so dramatically among Japanese-Americans for several related reasons. In the first place, generation is of special importance among Japanese-Americans (see Lyman, 1972). Because the period of immigration was so short, roughly from 1890 to 1920, the Issei were almost like a single birth cohort, moving through their careers together. Their children, the Nisei, were more spread out in age, but they tended to see themselves as a single group, different from the Issei and similar to each other in important ways. In turn, their children, the Sansei, are even more spread out in age, but are seen as being generally distinct from the Nisei in their values and behavior. Each of these generations experienced a unique pattern of events and is thought to exhibit a correspondingly identifiable character.

The Sansei are the first generation to intermarry in large numbers partly because they are the first generation to grow up free of the pressure of blatant discrimination. Relatively few of the Nisei in the continental United States intermarried because, when they came of age, many intermarriages were prohibited by law or, regardless of the marriage laws, they found themselves in "relocation camp"—hardly a likely place to find a non-Japanese spouse. Considering the effects of these events on all but the youngest Nisei, it is not surprising that their intermarriage rate was low. These external pressures preventing intermarriage have largely disappeared as the Sansei have reached maturity. The laws against intermarriage have disappeared and for a variety of reasons, the virulent prejudice which the Issei and the older Nisei experienced has abated. In fact, it has been replaced by a widely-held positive image of the Japanese (Sue and Kitano, 1973). In part, therefore, the increased intermarriage rate can be seen as a consequence of changes in the discriminatory practices of the dominant society.

In addition to this, a second important change has been taking place at the same time. Not only have the pressures against intermarriage imposed by the dominant society been relaxed as the Sansei grew up, but the Sansei themselves are different from their parents in their attitudes and beliefs. In fact, each succeeding Japanese-American generation shows greater acculturation, greater approval of interaction with Caucasians, and a higher rate of interaction across the race line (Woodrum, 1978:80). Woodrum reports, among the Nisei, a mixed, or even bimodal, pattern of acculturation and assimilation (1978:84). That is, while they speak English fluently, many of them also speak Japanese well. Slightly over half of them identify themselves as

Christian while 37 percent retain traditional Japanese religious affiliations. And, finally although the Nisei in general report having roughly equal proportions of Japanese and Caucasian friends, 39 percent of them have over two-thirds of their group memberships in primarily Japanese-American organizations while 45 percent indicate that fewer than one-third of their memberships are in primarily Japanese groups (Woodrum, 1978:84). While the Nisei show this mixed pattern of adaptation, their children generally show much greater acculturation and assimilation. The Sansei are less likely than their parents to be able to speak Japanese, more likely to participate chiefly in mixed voluntary associations, and more likely to report having Caucasians as closest friends. Just as Gordon's model predicts, the high rate of marital assimilation among the Sansei has followed, in an orderly fashion, the increasing cultural and structural assimilation of their parents and of their own generation.

Social Class

Although Woodrum's data clearly show a regular increase, with each generation, in acculturation and assimilation, they also indicate that some individuals are more likely to assimilate than others. Montero and Tsukashima (1977), working with the same Japanese-American research project data that Woodrum analyzed, find evidence which sheds additional light on the increasing rate of intermarriage among the Sansei. In the first place, they find that although few of the Sansei's parents themselves intermarried (less than 10 percent), a high proportion of them do not disapprove of intermarriage. In fact, 59.3 percent of them report that they are not disturbed by intermarriage. Secondly, they find that a reasonably good predictor of the attitudes of the Nisei respondents toward intermarrriage is their education. That is, respondents with higher educations tend to be more accepting about intermarriage. In addition, the more highly educated Nisei are more acculturated and assimilated in many respects. That is, they are less likely to speak Japanese, more likely to live in non-Japanese neighborhoods, and more likely to have co-workers and friends who are not Japanese (Montero and Tsukashima, 1977:497).

Levine and Montero (1973) find that educational differences among the Nisei are paralleled by more general socioeconomic class distinctions. The white collar and professional workers, those, generally with higher educations, are more likely to live in non-Japanese neighborhoods, and are less likely to belong to Japanese-American organizations. In addition, they are less likely to be able to speak Japanese, are much less likely to be Buddhists, and, finally, are less likely to disapprove of intermarriage. The data show that, among the Nisei, acculturation and assimilation are positively related to social class. After World War II, with the reduction of discrimination that occurred then, when a Nisei completed college or professional school, he or she tended to move into a white-collar or professional job in the mainstream of society. At the same time that this movement into the occupational mainstream occurred, the highly educated, white-collar Nisei tended to move away from the Japanese community and Japanese values in other ways. Levine and Montero (1973:44) conclude that it is reasonable to divide the Nisei into two strata: a relatively assimilated, urban white-collar stratum whose members approve of intermarriage (although they are not, themselves, intermarried) and a much less assimilated blue-collar or rural stratum.

In the case of the Sansei, this division is less clear. They are vigorously pursuing higher education: in 1967, when the Japanese-American Research Project data were gathered, 88 percent of the Sansei had at least some college training (Levine and Montero, 1973:45). Those who had not completed college were generally in the process of completing a degree and an astonishing 92 percent of the Sansei intended to become professionals. It seems very likely that, pursuing their educational and occupational goals, the Sansei, like their highly educated Nisei parents, will be drawn away from the Japanese community, into the larger society. In this light, it becomes easier to understand the very high rate of intermarriage that we observed among the Sansei (above). In fact, this opens the possibility that this generation and the next (if their children continue this process) will assimilate so thoroughly that the Japanese community will wither away.

Religion

In addition to the social class differences discussed above, religion appears to be related to intermarriage rates. Levine and Montero found that the less assimilated Nisei, who were less likely to approve of intermarriage, were also predominantly Buddhist (1973:45). Intermarriage data from one California city show the same sort of thing. That is, virtually none (5 percent) of the Japanese who got married in Buddhist ceremonies in Fresno, California, intermarried while 58 percent of Japanese marrying in Christian ceremonies were intermarried (Tinker, 1972). This opens the possibility that, while many Japanese-Americans are assimilating, a core Japanese group, the Buddhists, may be maintaining their ethnic distinctiveness and defending their group boundaries. A hint of this is found in a very early paper by Miyamoto (1939) who reported that the Buddhists in Seattle were much more conservative and "Japanese" than the Christians. In order to assess the possibility that, among the Sansei in central California, the Buddhists form a less assimilated group which resists intermarriage, a survey of the attitudes of all Japanese-surnamed students at California State University, Fresno, was undertaken.

Building on the theoretical foundation provided by Gordon (1964), three general issues were investigated in this survey: cultural assimilation, structural assimilation, and interracial dating. The items which were meant to tap cultural assimilation are concerned with such things as the importance of maintaining Japanese traditions, being able to speak or understand Japanese, and knowing the history of Japan. If the Buddhists actually form a separate community, culturally different from the rest of the Sansei, if they are less likely to assimilate, these questions should reveal significant differences between the Buddhists and the non-Buddhists (Christians and those who declare no religion). In fact, however, there are no significant differences between Buddhists and others on any of these items. However important the religious distinction may have been among the Nisei, among these Sansei college students, it does not seem to be crucial; at least not with respect to these specifically cultural items.

A second collection of items focussed on structural assimilation. In general, these questions were concerned with choosing mostly Japanese friends, seeking to do business with Japanese professionals and tradesmen, and belonging to Japanese organizations. If the Buddhists form a distinct community, socially apart from the rest of the society, these questions should reveal it. Again, however, no significant differences appear between the Buddhists and the non-Buddhists. Among these Sansei respondents, religion does not mark off a separate ethnic structure.

Finally, they were asked about interracial dating. This, of course, is most clearly related to marriage and may be taken as the most direct prediction of intermarriage trends in the near future. Remember that other studies have found that, among the Nisei, Buddhists were much less likely than non-Buddhists to approve intermarriage and, correspondingly they appeared much less likely to intermarry. If these attitudes have been transmitted to their Sansei children, we would expect the Buddhists to be different from the others in the extent to which they interdate and in the attitudes they have toward interracial dating. The data do not show these differences, however. Far more than fifty percent of both religious groups indicate that they have interdated. In fact, of those responding to the question, 65 percent of the Buddhists and 78 percent of the others say that they have dated Caucasians. This suggests that the religious boundary, which was a significant cultural and social marker in the last generation, is losing its force now; that university-educated Sansei (recall that earlier studies have shown almost 90 percent of the Sansei to have come college education) are assimilating culturally, structurally, and many of them seem willing to make the final step to marital assimilation.

Sex Ratio

Another aspect of the pattern of intermarriages in the United States is that almost all of the studies show that women predominate among the Japanese who intermarry. The summary of studies in Table 3 shows how pervasive this pattern has been. Looking first at the studies done in the continental United States, only one shows a higher proportion of males than females among those intermarrying. In fact, the census data indicate that, of all the intermarriages found in the decade 1940–49 and surviving until the census day in 1969, 72.2 percent were marriages of Japanese females. Among the surviving intermarriages formed in 1950–59, 94 percent involved Japanese females and 75.3 percent of those formed from 1960–1969 involved Japanese females (U.S. Bureau of the Census, 1972). The data from Hawaii (see Table 3) also show a consistent predominance of females among those who intermarry, although the ratio is never so disproportionate as it has been at times on the mainland.

There have been several explanations for the unbalanced sex ratio in these intermarriages. The first is that a radically unbalanced sex ratio in a group can encourage intermarriage, because some members will have to go outside the group to find mates and therefore the pattern of intermarriage will necessarily be sexually imbalanced.

TABLE 3

SEX OF JAPANESE SPOUSE IN INTERMARRIAGE BY DECADE
AND REGION

	Number of Intermarriages	Males (%)	Females (%)
1940-49			
United States, 1940-49[1]	4,362	1,213 (27.8%)	3,149 (72.2%)
Los Angeles, 1949[2]	20	8 (40%)	12 (60%)
1950-59			
United States (less Hawaii),[1] 1950-59	17,500	1,115 (6%)	16,385 (94%)
California, 1955-59[2]	1,030	355 (34.5%)	675 (65.5%)
Los Angeles, 1950-59[2]	576	197 (34%)	379 (66%)
1960-69			
United States (less Hawaii),[1] 1960-69	18,239	4,511 (24.7%)	13,728 (75.3%)
Los Angeles, 1960-61[3]	345	98 (28.4%)	247 (71.6%)
Fresno, CA, 1960-69[4]	79	46 (58.2%)	33 (41.8%)
1970-			
Los Angeles, 1971-72[2]	551	223 (40.5%)	328 (59.5%)
Fresno, CA, 1970-71[4]	41	19 (46.3%)	22 (53.7%)
Hawaii,[5] 1920-30	480	223 (46%)	257 (54%)
1930-40	1,086	435 (40%)	651 (60%)
1940-49	3,489	631 (18%)	2,858 (82%)
1950-59	4,691	1,349 (29%)	3,342 (71%)
1960-69	6,796	2,617 (38.5%)	4,179 (61.5%)

1. U.S. Bureau of the Census: 1970, Table 12
2. Kikumura & Kitano: 1973, Table 1
3. Burma et al.: 1970, Table 1
4. Tinker: 1973, Table 1
5. Glick, C.: 1970, Recalculated from Table 1

This has been mentioned by a number of students of intermarriage. For instance, it is the chief factor discussed by Kikumura and Kitano (1973) when they consider the ratio of females to males among intermarrying Japanese (see also Glick, 1970; Cheng and Yamamura, 1957). They point out that, according to the census, there were slightly more Japanese males than females in Fresno, California, where males predominated in intermarriage, while there were more females than males in both San Francisco and Los Angeles, where females were in the majority among those intermarrying. This explanation undoubtedly has some validity, especially when the sex ratio in a group is radically out of balance among those in the prime age for marriage. According to Kikumura and Kitano (1973) there were 271,300 Japanese males and 319,900 Japanese females in the United States in 1970. Females were in the majority, but they were only 54 percent of the total and some part of that majority had to be made up of surviving widows who did not see themselves in the marriage market.

This imbalance in the sex ratio is simply not large enough to account by itself for the striking over-representation of Japanese females in intermarriages during the last thirty years in the United States.

A second explanation, which is likely to be most important for the 1945–1960 period, is the war-bride phenomenon. A large number of American military personnel, most of them Caucasian, married Japanese women while they were stationed in Japan after World War II. For the whole period from 1945 to 1970, there are reported to have been 55,456 Japanese war-brides (Kim, 1972:273; see also Schnepp and Yui, 1956; Strauss, 1954). These marriages undoubtedly account for some part, and possibly in some decades a large part, of the unbalanced sex ratio in Japanese intermarriages. In fact they may account for the really astonishing disproportion of females among the Japanese who intermarried in the 1940s, 50s, and 60s (for the continental United States, 72.2 percent, 94 percent, and 75.3 percent). Table 3 appears to show a reducing disproportion in the sex ratio (down from the high of 94 percent females in the 1950s) and that may be very largely a result of a diminishing number of brides returning with American servicemen from Japan.

This still leaves a weaker, but noticeable, pattern of female predominance among the intermarried as can be seen in Table 3. This is interesting because many studies have shown that the males of most minorty groups marry out more frequently than the females (Barnett, 1963; Merton, 1941; van den Berghe, 1960). Why has this pattern been reversed among the Japanese-Americans? Several reasons have been advanced to account for this (Tiner, 1973). Males were very important and privileged in the traditional Japanese family. They, especially the eldest son, were responsible for carrying on the family line. This responsibility might have discouraged them from making nontraditional marriages. In addition, males had a position of advantage in the traditionally patriarchal Japanese family. In keeping with this tradition, Nisei and even Sansei males hold more male-dominant views than do Caucasian males their age (Arkoff, Meredith, and Dong, 1963). Japanese-American females, on the other hand, have been much quicker to acculturate in this regard. They are not different from their Caucasian age-mates with respect to ideas about male dominance. Kitano has remarked that the Japanese-American family tends still to be male-dominated, with women in a subordinate position. "The Japanese-American female obviously resents this position, and many marital conflicts arise from these differences in expectation" (Kitano, 1969:66). Part of the over-representation of Japanese-American females among those intermarrying may thus be a consequence of their more rapid acculturation, leading them to seek mates with similar family values. If this is the case, we would expect the sex ratio to slowly come into balance as more widespread and complete acculturation occurs among the males as well.

Conclusion

We have seen that the intermarriage rate is very high, ranging up to 50 percent of all the marriages of Japanese in the continental United States. Moreover, this has been shown to be a reliable finding, one which appears in a number of studies done

72   *INTERMARRIAGE IN THE UNITED STATES*

in many specific locations as well as being reflected in the broader national census data. This is an extraordinary finding in the light of the general disapproval of racial intermarriage revealed by national polls. Its implications for this society and for the Japanese-American minority in the United States are very important.

In the first place, it provides evidence of the thorough assimilation of the Japanese-Americans. Milton Gordon's widely cited model of assimilation postulates that intermariage is the final stage of assimilation of a minority group. The first stage is cultural assimilation, then structural assimilation, then, finally, marital assimilation. In the case of the Japanese-Americans, the evidence suggests that these stages, in this order, describe their history over the last three generations. The detailed studies which we reviewed (especially Levine and Montero, 1973; Montero and Tsukashima, 1977; Kikumura and Kitano, 1973; Tinker, 1972, 1973; and Woodrum, 1978) indicate that the Nisei who approve of intermarriage are generally those who, by their religion, education, occupation, place of residence, and friendship patterns, appear to be the most culturally and structurally assimilated. These data also show that the Sansei who interdate and intermarry are thoroughly assimilated. This indicates that Japanese-Americans are moving through Gordon's stages of assimilation in very much the same way that many European immigrant groups have before them. That does not mean that they will necessarily disappear or be forgotten. Just as completely assimilated decendents of immigrants from Scotland or France claim their heritage, so we can expect the descendents of Japanese immigrants to be proud of their families' accomplishments. The evidence shows that the Sansei, even those who intermarry, are not trying to deny their past; their intermarriage is just the natural expression of their dispersion into the large society (Levine and Montero, 1973).

In the continental United States, this high rate of intermarriage may signal the withering away of Japanese institutions and the eventual practical disappearance of the Japanese community. The Japanese minority is so small, compared to the surrounding society, that this high rate of intermarriage, accompanied by occupational and residential dispersion, is likely to mean that the Japanese, while still proud of their heritage, will be unable to maintain a distinctive Japanese community. In Hawaii, the situation is different. Even though the intermarriage rate is high, the Japanese minority is so large that aspects of a Japanese community such as churches, social groups, shops, and residential enclaves may be maintained for a long time.

While the implications of this high intermarriage rate for the Japanese minority are obviously significant, the implications for the whole society are no less important. The United States has been characterized as an unalterably racist society; a colonial and imperialist society in which non-white groups are denied, because of their color, full participation. There is no denying the history of racism in this society, but the question is whether race, by itself, with class and cultural barriers removed, must remain a boundary between American people. The Japanese example suggests that the answer is "no." The Japanese suffered sever hostility, culminating in relocation during World War II, the harshest official act of discrimination in modern United States history, but this review of intermarriage research has shown that the racial boundary which set them off from the majority society is such a dramatic way a generation ago has not remained permanent. The United States has been a racist society, but this example suggests that it is not doomed forever to remain one.

REFERENCES

Adams, Romanzo. *Interracial Marriage in Hawaii.* New York: The Macmillan Company, 1937.

Arkoff, A., Meredith, G. and J. Dong. "Attitudes of Japanese-American and Caucasian-American students toward marriage roles." *Journal of Social Psychology*, 1963, *49*:11-15.

Barnett, Larry D. "Interracial marriage in California." *Marriage and Family Living*, 1963, *25*:425-427.

Blauner, Robert. *Racial Oppression in America.* New York: Harper and Row, 1972.

Burma, John H. "Interethnic marriage in Los Angeles, 1948-59." *Social Forces*, 1963, *42*:156-165.

Burma, John H., Gary A. Cretser, and Ted Seacrest. "A comparison of the occupational status of intramarrying and intermarrying couples: A research note." *Sociology and Social Research*, 1970, *54*:508-519.

Cheng, C. K., and Douglas S. Yamamura. "Interracial marriage and divorce in Hawaii." *Social Forces*, 1957, *36*:77-84.

Conner, John W. "Acculturation and family continuities in three generations of Japanese Americans." *Journal of Marriage and the Family*, 1974, *36*:159-165.

Erlich, Howard J. *The Social Psychology of Prejudice.* New York: John Wiley and Sons, 1973.

Gallup, George. *The Gallup Poll: Public Opinion 1972-1977.* Wilmington, DE: Scholarly Resources, Inc., 1978.

Glick, Clarence E. "Interracial marriage and admixture in Hawaii." *Social Biology*, 1970, *17*:248-291.

Glick, Paul C. "Intermarriage among ethnic groups in the United States." *Social Biology*, 1970, *17*:292-298.

Gordon, Milton M. *Assimilation in American Life.* New York: Oxford University Press, 1964.

Greeley, Andrew M. and Paul B. Sheatsley. "Attitudes toward racial integration." In L. Rainwater (ed.), *Social Problems and Public Policy: Inequality and Justice.* Chicago: Aldine Publishing Co., 1974, 241-250.

Gurak, Douglas T., and Mary M. Kritz. "Intermarriage patterns in the U.S.: Maximizing information from the U.S. Census public use samples." *Public Data Use*, March 1978: 33-43.

Kikumura, Akemi, and Harry H. L. Kitano. "Interracial marriage: A Picture of the Japanese Americans." *Journal of Social Issues*, 1973, *29*:67-82.

Kim, Bok-Lim C. "Casework with Japanese and Korean wives of Americans." *Social Casework*, 1972, *53*:273-279.

Kitano, Harry H. L. *Japanese-Americans: The Evolution of a Subculture.* Englewood Cliffs, NJ: Prentice-Hall, 1969.

Leon, Joseph J. "Sex-Ethnic marriage in Hawaii: A nonmetric multidimensional analysis." *Journal of Marriage and the Family*, 1975, *37*:775-781.

Levine, Gene N., and Darrel M. Montero. "Socioeconomic mobility among three generations of Japanese Americans." *Journal of Social Issues* 1973, *29*:33-48.

Lind, Andrew. *Hawaii's People.* Honolulu: University of Hawaii Press, 1967.

Lyman, Stanford M. "Generation and character: The case of the Japanese Americans." In Hilary Conroy and T. Scott Miyakawa (eds.), *East Across the Pacific.* Santa Barbara, CA: Clio Press, 1972, 279-314.

Merton, Robert K. "Intermarriage and social structure: Fact and theory." *Psychiatry*, 1941, *4*:361-374.

Miyamota, S. Frank. "Social solidarity among the Japanese in Seattle." *University of Washington Publications in the Social Sciences*, 1939, *11*:57-130.

74   *INTERMARRIAGE IN THE UNITED STATES*

Montero, Darrel, and Ronald Tsukashima. "Assimilation and educational achievement: The case of the second generation Japanese-American." *The Sociological Quarterly*, 1977, *18*:490–503.

Omatsu, G. "Nihonmachi Beat." *Hokubei Mainichi*, January 12, 1972.

Parkman, Margaret A., and Jack Sawyer. "Dimensions of ethnic intermarriage in Hawaii." *American Sociological Review*, 1967, *32*:593–607.

Schmitt, Robert. "Demographic correlates of interracial marriage in Hawaii." *Demography*, 1964, *2*:463–473.

Schnepp, Gerald J., and Agnes Masako Yui. "Cultural and marital adjustment of Japanese war brides." *American Journal of Sociology*, 1956, *61*:48–50.

Simpson, George E., and J. Milton Yinger. *Racial and Cultural Minorities: An Analysis of Prejudice and Discrimination*. New York: Harper and Row, 1958.

Simpson, George E., and J. Milton Yinger. *Racial and Cultural Minorities: An Analysis of Prejudice and Discrimination*. Fourth Edition. New York: Harper and Row, 1972.

Strauss, Anselm L. "Strain and harmony in American-Japanese war-bride marriages." *Marriage and Family Living*, 1954, *16*:99–106.

Sue, Stanley, and Harry H. L. Kitano. "Stereotypes as a measure of success." *Journal of Social Issues*, 1973, *29*:83–98.

Sue, Stanley, Derald Sue, and David W. Sue. "Asian Americans as a minority group." *American Psychologist*, 1975, *30*:906–910.

Tinker, John N. "The penetration of group boundries: Intermarriage and religion among Japanese-Americans." Paper presented at the meetings of the Society for the Study of Social Problems, New Orleans, Louisiana, 1972.

Tinker, John N. "Intermarriage and ethnic boundaries: The Japanese American case." *Journal of Social Issues*, 1973, *29*:49–66.

U.S. Bureau of the Census. Census of Population: 1970. Marital Status, Final Report PC(2)-4C Washington, D.C.: U.S. Government Printing Office, 1972.

van den Berghe, Pierre. "Hypergamy, hypergenation, and miscegenation." *Human Relations*, 1960, *13*:83–91.

Woodrum, Eric Marc. "Japanese American Social Adaptation Over Three Generations." Ph.D. dissertation, University of Texas at Austin, 1978.

KOREAN INTERRACIAL MARRIAGE

Harry H.L. Kitano
Lynn Kyung Chai

There is a paucity of material on Korean interracial marriage. During our study, we asked a number of Asian Americans their general opinion as to Korean interracial marriage rates, and aside from those who professed ignorance, the other most common response was that it was high, based partially on impressions from Hawaii. Part of the reason for the general ignorance about Korean interracial marriage is the scarcity of written work about the Koreans in general, which in part is based on their relatively small numbers and the newness of their migration.

The purpose of this study is to present data on Korean interracial marriage in Los Angeles, the center of the Korean population in the United States. Generalizations concerning the Los Angeles population should be modified for other areas of the country since relative size and the cohesion of an ethnic community are known to be related to the marital patterns of any ethnic group.

Background

Before presenting the data from our study, we will present background material on one of America's least known Asian groups. Korean migration to the United States has been characterized by several distinct stages, and each movement has contributed to different types of marital and family patterns.

There was an initial immigration of young Koreans to work on Hawaii's plantations in the early part of the century; the aftermath of the Korean War (1950–53) brought an influx of refugees and war brides, while the Immigration Act of 1965 has resulted in a steady flow of new immigrants. The last immigration has been and continues to be a relatively heavy one, so that Koreans are known as one of the fastest growing Asian groups (the Filipino is the other) in the United States (Kim, 1980:601). In the 1980 census, their population was 354,529, which placed them as the fourth most numerous Asian group behind the Chinese, Filipino and the Japanese.

Each of these groups is different, although the early group faced much more prejudice, racism, and discrimination than the newer immigrants. For example interracial marriage between Koreans (and other Asians and non-whites) to whites was

Harry H.L. Kitano, Ph.D., is affiliated with the Departments of Social Welfare and Sociology, U.C.L.A. Lynn Kyung Chai is a Graduate Student in the Department of Social Welfare, U.C.L.A. The authors wish to thank the Ford Foundation, the Institute of American Cultures, and the Asian American Studies Center at UCLA for funding the research.

legally prohibited in California until 1958. The most important generalization is that the Koreans are not a homogeneous group, and that these rough divisions are related to different family and marital patterns.

First Immigration

Although there were a few students who arrived in America in 1885, the first signficant migration of Koreans took place between 1902 and 1905. The numbers were small, under 10,000, and the great majority were young males recruited to work on the sugar plantations in Hawaii. Further migration ceased for a number of reasons. Korea was made a protectorate of Japan in 1905 by the treaty of Kanghwa, and the Japanese closed the Korean Emigration Office and forbade further immigration to the United States. The Gentleman's Agreement of 1907 designed to restrict the flow of Japanese laborers to the United States also included Korean laborers, and the racially motivated 1924 Immigration Act closed the door to all Asian immigration. All of these actions served to isolate the initial small band of Korean immigrants. The only exception was the almost 1000 Korean females, known as "picture brides" because their primary contact with their prospective grooms was through the exchange of pictures, who arrived in Hawaii and California between 1910 and 1924 (Kim, 1980).

The United States Census recorded the number of Koreans in Hawaii as follows: 1910, 4533; 1920, 4950; 1930, 6461, and 1940, 6851. The numbers on the mainland were even smaller; in 1910, 461; 1920, 1677; 1930, 1860; and 1940, 1711.

There were a number of interrelated factors about this immigrant group which made their second generation American born children especially prone to outmarriage. The Koreans did not develop a close, ethnic community, rather they were highly dispersed; they placed a heavy emphasis on acculturation and learning the American way; they placed high expectations on education and the achievement of professional status. Finally, their population was much too small to maintain intra-ethnic marital choices.

As one consequence, the decendants from these original immigrants are described as having one of the highest interethnic marriage rates in Hawaii. During the period between 1960-68, 80 percent of the Korean brides and grooms married non-Koreans in comparison to the 40 percent outmariage rates for other ethnic groups covering the same period. The outmarrying Korean brides tended to prefer Caucasian grooms while the outmarrying Korean males tended to prefer Japanese females (Harvey and Chung, 1980:135). Therefore the general impression that Korean interracial marriage is high in Hawaii is confirmed by the data.

One of the prices paid by this Korean group in Hawaii for rapid acculturation and the achievement of middle-class status has been that of high divorce rates. Harvey and Chung (1980:135) write that the Koreans are the highest in the category of households headed by women suggesting a high incidence of divorce. In summary, the early immigrants, their second generation American born children and the third generation have been characterized by high rates of outmarriage. Although the generalizations are based on data from Hawaii, it is assumed that since similar conditions prevailed on the mainland the same marital patterns probably occurred. Data on the mainland Koreans are lacking (Korean data prior to the forthcoming 1980 Census has generally been lumped together with other small groups under "other"), but the extremely small and scattered population on the mainland may indicate an even higher rate of outmarriage.

The Refugees and War Brides

The second distinctive group of Korean immigrants came to the United States between 1952 and 1960. These included over 20,000 refugees of which the great majority were "war brides" and the children of American servicemen (Kim, 1980:601). Possible conflicts in these intercultural marriages are analyzed by Ratliff, Moon and Bonacci (1978). They mention that most marriages in Korea are arranged by the parents and that many of these wartime marriages apparently did not go through the parental sanctioning procedures. The feeling that many of these brides were prostitutes was also strongly held, and it is probable that some of these negative feelings still remain in Korean communities in America. In 72.9 percent of the cases of the war brides that were studied, the Korean women responded that they had married because of financial reasons and 68 percent answered that they would not marry an American serviceman again (Ratliff et al., 1978:221). Further information about this group is difficult to find, especially after their arrival in the United States. There is a general impression that a high percentage of the war bride marriages have ended in divorce but empirical evidence to substantiate these impressions is unavailable.

The Major Immigration

The current immigration can be classified as the major Korean migration to the United States. The population movement began in the late 1960s and by 1970, approximately 20,000 Koreans were arriving and settling on the mainland yearly, with many choosing Los Angeles (Kim, 1980). As a result the approximately 5000 Koreans recorded in Los Angeles in 1970 had grown to an estimated 150,000[1] by the late 1970s earning the City of Angels the name of the Korean capital in the United States.

The Immigration Act of 1965 which became effective in 1968 was a major factor in lifting the barriers to Korean emigration. The majority of the new immigrants have been young females between 20-39 years of age (Kim, 1980:604). Bok-Lim Kim and Cordon (1975) found in a Chicago study the following reasons for immigration: 1) to gain a better education, 2) to obtain better employment and 3) to be reunited with their family and other relatives.

The new immigrants have developed a Korean community. For example, in Los Angeles, Sherman (1979) writes that many have immigrated with money and education so that "Koreatown" has 5 shopping centers, 10 small strip shopping centers,

---

[1]The estimates of Koreans in Los Angeles range from 60,000 to 150,000.

30 Korean restaurants, 5 supermarkets, 10 nightclubs, 80 churches, 4 Buddhist temples, 3 clinics and several schools. They have developed a reputation for being dynamic and aggressive in business. Cha (1977) sees a cultural assimilation, but very little structural or identificational assimilation. Rather, the Korean community appears largely independent of American society.

Kim (1977) summarizes some of the social characteristics of the Koreans who have arrived in the U.S. since the 1965 Immigration Act. They plan to stay in the United States permanently (although the relative ease of air travel makes frequent trips easy); they are unfamiliar with the United States; a major barrier is the English language which forces a high dependence on the ethnic community; they are highly educated but their education and training is difficult to translate into equivalent jobs in the United States (i.e., high school and college teachers, priests and ministers). A large number go into private business but the move may be attributed more to limited opportunities and therefore be symbols of disguised poverty, rather than profitable free enterprise entrepreneurship.

Data, Source and Findings

Our current study focusses on the marital patterns of the new immigrants who have arrived in what we have titled the major migration.

Our primary source for data was the Los Angeles County Marriage License Bureau. We checked the marriage application index and drew out every Korean surname for 1975, 1977, and 1979. The surname itself, the birthplace of the applicant and the birthplace of the applicant's parents, as well as the name of the father and maiden name of the mother provided clues as to nationality. The research team included individuals familiar with Chinese, Japanese and Korean surnames (there are many similarities between Chinese and Korean surnames). Any marriage outside the Korean group was considered an outmarriage.

Los Angeles is currently thought of as the "Korean capital" of the United States and it is presumed that the figures are the largest among Koreans in the United States.

There are two other plausible sites that Los Angeles Koreans (as well as from other areas) frequently use for marriage. One alternative is to get married in Las Vegas or some other city in Nevada, and it is our impression that a high proportion of these unions are outmarriages. The other practice is to go back to Korea for a bride or groom and since this procedure virtually guarantees an inmarriage, these two options may balance each other in terms of in-and outmarriages.

Findings

A. Outmarriage

The data concerning rates of Korean in and outmarriage for 1975, 1977, and 1979 are presented in Table I. In 1975 there were 250 Korean marriages of which 26.0 percent were to non-Koreans; in 1977 there were 232 marriages of which 34.1 percent were to non-Koreans, and in 1979, there were 334 marriages of which 27.6 per-

TABLE I

Korean Outmarriage by Total and by Sex,
Los Angeles County, 1979, 1977, 1975

| Year | Total Korean Marriages | Total Outmarriage | | Outmarriage | | | |
| | | N | % | Male | | Female | |
				N	%	N	%
1979	333	92	27.6	19	20.4	73	79.6
1977	232	79	34.1	21	26.6	58	73.4
1975	250	65	26.0	24	36.9	41	63.1

cent were to non-Koreans. Therefore in terms of rates, there is no apparent trend in terms of upward or downward, rather there are similar rates for 1975 and 1979, with a slightly higher rate in 1977.

However, there are trends when we analyze the data by sex (Table I). In 1975, 63.1 percent of the Korean females married non-Koreans; in 1977, 73.4 percent married non-Koreans while in 1979, 79.6 percent married non-Koreans. Conversely, there is a decreasing trend among Korean males; in 1975 36.9 percent married non-Koreans; in 1977 26.6 percent married non-Koreans and in 1979, 20.4 percent married non-Koreans. Therefore our data shows that Korean females outmarry at a higher rate than males and the rates appear to be increasing, whereas the rate and trend for the Korean males is in the opposite direction.

Interracial Marriages. Table I showed the outmarriage rate of Koreans to non-Koreans. Table II shows the outmarriages to Chinese, Japanese and to non-Asian spouses. Marriages to non-Asians constitutes our rate of interracial marriage.

In 1975, 73.8 percent of Korean marriages were to non-Asians; in 1977, 78.5 percent of Korean marriages were to non-Asians and in 1979, 69.6 percent of the Koreans married non-Asians.

B. Differences between the In and Outmarrieds

1. Age. Table III compares the age of the inmarried and outmarried Koreans by sex. There was a chi-square of 12.2 between the male groups and a chi-square of 11.4 between the female groups, both statistically significant at better than the .05 level.

The largest differences between the in-and outmarried males were in the 26 to 50 year old categories. The inmarriages were higher in the 26 to 30 (26.3 to 31.1 percent) and 31 to 40 year (26.3 to 34.8 percent) old categories while the outmarrieds were higher in the 41 to 50 (21.1 to 9.6 percent) year old category. In general the males who outmarry tend to be older than the Korean males who chose Korean brides.

TABLE II

Ethnicity of Non-Korean Spouse

Year	Total Outmarriage N	Chinese N	%	Japanese N	%	Other* N	%
1979	92	12	13	16	17.4	64	69.6
1977	79	8	10.1	9	11.4	62	78.5
1975	65	6	9.2	11	16.9	48	73.8

* Non-Asian surname, presumed to be white.

TABLE III

Differences Between Male and Female in and
Outmarried Koreans by Age

		Males* (Percent)		Females* (Percent)	
		Out (N=19)	In (N=241)	Out (N=73)	In (N=241)
1.	Age:* Under 25	21.1	20.7	34.2	49.8
	26-30	26.3	31.1	34.2	28.6
	31-40	26.3	34.9	23.3	15.4
	41-50	21.1	9.6	8.2	3.3
	51 Over	5.3	3.7	0.0	2.9
Total		100.1	100	99.9	100

* Significant at the .05 level.

There were differences between the inmarried and outmarried females in almost every age category. The inmarried Korean females had almost one-half in the under 25 year old category, while the outmarried females had larger figures in all other categories except for the 51 or older category. The most appropriate generalization is that a high proportion of the younger Korean females tend to marry within the group. However, mean ages showed no significant differences. The inmarried male mean age was 32.2 years; the outmarried male was 33.6 years. The inmarried female mean age was 27.1 years; the outmarried mean age was 28.9 years.

2. *By generation.* The differences between the inmarried and outmarried Koreans by generations is shown on Table IV. By first generation we refer to those Koreans born in Korea and arriving in the United States as immigrants; the second generation are the children of immigrant parents while the 3rd generation (or more) refers to children born of American born parents.

The data clearly show the importance of generational differences between the inmarried and outmarried males. The chi-square of 73.6 is statistically significant. The great majority of inmarried males are of the first generation (98.8 percent) whereas the outmarried males are of the second and third generation.

The figures concerning generational differences are also true for the females. The chi-square of 15.9 between the inmarried and outmarried females is statistically significant. Generally first generation females tend to marry Korean grooms while second and third generation females are not as endogamous.

3. *By birthplace.* The differences between the inmarried and outmarried Koreans by birthplace is shown on Table V. The vast majority of inmarried Korean males were born in Korea (18.3 percent) whereas the outmarried Korean males were distributed between Korea (57.9 percent) and United States birthplaces (31.6 percent), with a small number also born in Japan (5.3). The chi-square of 72.8 is statistically significant.

A similar distribution was found among the females. The majority of inmarried Korean females were born in Korea (98.3 percent). Although there was also a high percentage of outmarried Korean brides born in Korea (83.6 percent), there were also a few born in the United States (8.2 percent) and in Japan (6.8 percent). The chi-square of 31.6 is statistically significant.

4. *Number of marriages.* The differences in the number of marriages between the inmarried and outmarried Koreans is shown on Table VI. There is a tendency

TABLE IV

Differences in Generation Between
Inmarried and Outmarried Koreans by Sex

	Generation of Groom*	Percent Out (N=19)	In (N=241)	Generation of Bride*	Percent Out (N=73)	In (N=241)
1st		63.2	98.8		91.8	99.6
2nd		10.5	1.2		2.7	0.0
3rd or More		26.4			5.5	0.4
Total		100.1	100.1		100.0	100.0

Chi-square = 7.36*   Chi-square = 15.9*

* Significant at the .05 level.

TABLE V

Difference by Birthplace of Spouse Between
Inmarried and Outmarried Koreans by Sex

Birthplace of Groom* N=19	Percent		Birthplace of Bride* N=54	Percent	
	Out (N=19)	In (N=241)		Out (N=73)	In (N=241)
Japan	5.3	.8		6.8	1.2
Korea	57.9	98.3		83.6	98.3
U.S.	31.6	.8		8.2	0.0
Other	5.2	0.0		1.4	.4
Total	100.1	99.9		100.0	99.9

Chi-square = 72.0*   Chi-square = 31.6*

* Significant at the .05 level.

among the Korean outmarried males to have been married more than once. The chi-square of 13.53 is statistically significant.

A similar but non-statistically significant picture (chi-square 5.3) is seen among the Korean females. The overall impression is the relatively high number of multiple marriages in the Los Angeles Korean population.

5. *Education.* The differences in education between the outmarried and inmarried Koreans is shown in Table VII. The major difference between the outmarried and inmarried males is in the high school graduate level (47.4 percent to 24.1 percent) and in higher education. The outmarried Korean male is likely to be a high school graduate while the inmarried Korean male is likely to have some college, to be a college graduate or to attend graduate school. The chi-square of 17.46 is statistically significant.

The picture for the Korean female is different. There is little difference between the outmarried and inmarried Korean female in education. The chi-square of 2.6 is not statistically significant. It is probable that variables other than education (i.e., attractiveness) is important in the choice of a bride.

C. Profile of the Non-Korean Married to the Korean

A profile of the non-Korean male and the non-Korean female married to the Korean is drawn from Table VIII. The variables include age, generation, number of marriages, birthplace, and years of education.

The male picture is as follows: the modal age is between 31-40 years of age; 54

percent are third generation or more Americans but a surprisingly high number (40.5 percent) were first generation immigrants. A relatively large percentage of these grooms were born in China and Japan (17.8 percent); the category of "other" (30.1 percent) included Latin Americans, Canadians, and a small number of Europeans. The majority of the grooms were in their first marriage (61.6 percent) however 30.1 percent were in their second and 8.2 percent were in their third marriage. The modal educational category was that of high school graduate (34.2 percent). However, combining the some college and above categories (60.2 percent) indicates that the non-Korean groom is generally well educated.

The profile of the non-Korean female married to the Korean male is drawn from Table VIII. Her modal age is under 25 (36.8 percent); she is likely to be of the first generation (52.6 percent) or of the third generation (42.1 percent) and 15.8 percent were born in China and Japan. The "other" category (31.6 percent) included Latin Americans, Canadians, and Europeans. The modal educational category was that of high school graduate (36.8 percent) with another 47.4 percent in the some college and above category.

There were a number of other variables that were studied such as when and how the last marriage ended; occupations and the birthplace of the fathers and mothers of the married couples. These variables did not provide any important information for the purposes of this article.

TABLE VI

Differences by Number of Marriage Between
Inmarried and Outmarried Koreans by Sex

| | Male* | | | Female | |
	Out (N=19)	In (N=241)		Out (N=73)	In (N=241)
N=19			N=54		
Marriages					
1st	63.2	70.5		69.9	77.6
2nd	31.6	26.6		26.0	19.5
3rd	0.0	2.9		4.1	2.9
4th or More	5.3	0.0		0.0	0.0
Total	100.1	100		100	100

Number of this Marriage (by Percent)

Chi-square = 13.5*   Chi-square = 1.8

* Significant at the .05 level.

TABLE VII

Differences in Education Between
Inmarried and Outmarried Koreans by Sex

Year of Education	Males* (by Percent)		Females	
	Out (N=19)	In (N=241)	Out (N=73)	In (N=241)
Grade School	0	1.2	2.7	3.3
Some High School	10.5	.8	4.1	3.7
High School Grad	47.4	24.1	37.0	31.5
Some College	10.5	18.3	23.3	29.5
College Grad	15.8	35.3	21.9	24.9
Graduate School	15.8	20.3	11.0	7.1
Total				
	100.0	100.0	100.0	100.0

Chi-square = 17.46*   Chi-sqaure = 2.6

* Significant at the .05 level.

Analysis and Discussion

Several generalizations can be drawn from our data. First, the Korean rates of outmarriage in Los Angeles County are low when compared to the rates reported in Hawaii (Harvy and Chung 1980) and are also low when compared to the Chinese (41 percent) and the Japanese (55 percent) in Los Angeles (study in progress). Secondly, the Korean female marries out of the group at a much higher rate than the Korean male. Part of the higher female rates can be attributed to the higher proportion of Korean females in the population. The practice of some males turning to brides in Korea is another factor.

Korean Family and Community

There are a number of factors concerning the Korean families and communities in the United States which provide the context for in and out-marriage. Chang (1977) stratifies the Korean families into three types: 1) the nativist who carries on traditional Korean family life, where the family is considered more important than the individual and where tradition and obedience are given high priority; 2) the assimilationist, who is more comfortable with American life styles; and 3) the bi-cultural family which recognizes the duality in their lives. It would be reasonable to assume that the lowest rates of outmarriage would come from the nativists, the highest rates from the assimilationists, with the bi-cultural group in between.

Kim, Bok-Lim (1980) develops some of the features of Korean adaptation to America. The majority arrive with a hard work, individualistic orientation and expect to achieve economic success. Nevertheless they retain certain aspects of the Korean culture, notably their language and have developed businesses which serve the Korean community.

TABLE VIII

Profile of Non-Korean Males and Females
Married to Koreans

	Non-Korean Male Married to Koreans (N=73) (by Percent)	Non-Korean Female Married to Koreans (N=19) (by Percent)
1. Age: Under 25	24.6	36.8
26-30	23.3	26.3
31-40	32.9	21.0
41-50	13.7	15.8
51 Over	5.5	
Total	100.0	99.9
2. Generation		
1st	40.5	52.6
2nd	5.5	5.2
3rd or More	54.0	42.1
Total	100.0	99.9
3. Birthplace		
Japan & China	17.8	15.8
Korea	0.0	15.8
U.S.	52.0	36.8
Other	30.1	31.6
Total	99.9	100.0
4. Number of Marriage		
1st	61.6	52.6
2nd	30.1	31.6
3rd or More	8.2	15.8
Total	99.9	100.0
5. Years of Education		
Grade School	0.0	0.0
Some High School	5.5	15.8
High School Grad	34.2	36.8
Some College	19.1	15.8
College Grad	19.1	15.8
Grad School	22.0	15.8
Total	99.9	100.0

For example, in Los Angeles, there is available a full range of community services ranging from ethnic newspapers, to Korean organizations such as community centers and churches, to interest groups, to small businesses and restaurants. The community is not as compact as the old "Chinatowns," but there are ample opportunities for Koreans to interact with other Koreans. There is also a tendency to relocate to the suburbs (and to live with the majority culture) as economic success is achieved.

Kim, B. (1980) suggests that certain trends appear to be emerging concerning Korean adaptation. On the one hand there is a rapid and aggressive move towards becoming a part of the mainstream in their economic lives, on the other, there is an attempt to retain a strong identification with the ethnic culture. Since much of their economic activities (i.e., car dealerships, service stations) are centered in the Korean community, such a bi-cultural adaptation is possible. As a consequence, Kim predicts that the group will choose neither of the extremes of total immersion in the ethnic subculture, nor the goals of complete acculturation. However, if the Korean immigrant follows the pattern of other immigrant groups, the American born second generation will probably choose a much more acculturative path. Even those Korean immigrants who arrived as children seem to have picked up American ways quickly, and given the discrepancies in power between the dominant and the ethnic group, such changes appear almost inevitable.

Generation

In our study, the most single important variable related to in and outmarriage was generation. The high rates of outmarriage in Hawaii were primarily second and third generation Koreans while the Los Angeles data, which shows a lower rate, addresses a first generation immigrant group. The traditional orientation towards marriage can be seen in an interview with a 53-year-old first generation mother: "I want my daughter to marry a nice Korean man and have (Korean) children."

The traditional orientation includes stigmatizing divorced women. Therefore, rates of outmarriage are related to the number of marriages (see Table VIII).

One Korean female, contemplating an outmarriage told us:

> I was divorced 4 years ago and I know it would be difficult to find a Korean man from a good family. The feelings of the community towards a divorced woman are very negative. It sounds unfair but the feelings are not strong towards the divorced man.

Parents still play an important role in arranging marriages. Divorced females are not considered as prime candidates by most traditional families.

Acculturation

Acculturation is the most important source of change for Korean families. Therefore the year of immigration creates its own system of stratification. An interview with a Korean female who married a Caucasian illustrates this factor.

We were one of the first Korean families to come to America in 1968. I was 20 years old at the time and there were almost no eligible Korean guys. I had to learn English and about America myself and I found that the Korean fellows who arrived later were too far behind me in speaking English and understanding this country.

Another female had similar feelings. Although still single, she has found difficulty in seriously dating Koreans who have recently immigrated. There are strains on traditional male and female roles (i.e., male dominant roles brought over from Korea), especially when the female is more knowledgeable about the American culture and has to assume the dominant role in a dating situation on such matters as what to order, where to go, and how to get there. One typology of the first generation Korean female likely to outmarry is as follows: a relatively early arrival (late 1960s and early 1970s) at an age where high school in Korea has already been completed. She therefore cannot go to high school in Los Angeles and the handicap of the English language is such that a college career is virtually closed, even though she may have gone to college in Korea. The number of eligible Korean males is small since the likelihood of interacting comfortably with the more newly arrived, less acculturated Korean male is low. The many Korean churches provide another important setting for those with a traditional orientation to meet each other and then there are the omnipresent Korean parents, continually searching for good marital prospects for their sons and daughters. There are also opportunities to meet other immigrant groups in beginning English and adult education classes which may account for the relatively high number of first generation Koreans marrying non-Koreans who are also of the first generation.

Number, Size and Sex Ratio

Another factor related to in and outmarriage is that of numbers. One Korean male currently a college professor and married to a Caucasian told us: "There just weren't any Korean females that I could date and get to know in the U.S. It was even more true on the East Coast where I went as a student."

The early immigrants and their descendents were a very small group so that expectations for inmarriage were unrealistic. One solution for these young males was the "picture brides," so that inmarriages were maintained by the first generation despite a shortage of Korean females in Hawaii. However, their children were also faced with a similar problem of small numbers and many of them opted for non-Korean spouses. There are now sufficient numbers of Koreans in Los Angeles to provide inmarriage possibilities.

In Group Cohesion

There are a number of factors which foster in-group cohesion and opportunities for in-group contact among Los Angeles Koreans. The community is geographically restricted so that rather than a scattered isolated group the majority of Koreans live in relative close proximity to each other and are held together by language, by cultural ties, by organizations and services, and by their general unfamiliarity with the dominant, English (or sometimes Spanish) speaking outside world. Cultural variables such as foods, and customs; family variables such as parental control and dependence on the family; community organizations such as the ethnic churches and community services foster a high in-group interaction which provides many opportunities for social contacts. One young, unmarried female told us, "There's lot of chances of meeting someone through the Korean church and at the university. It seems that we all know who the other Koreans are at UCLA (there are an estimated 500 Korean students at UCLA). I still haven't found anyone interesting yet, though."

Then there is the ever present variable of falling in love. The integrated work situation was the primary opportunity for interracial contact for this first generation female:

> I met my husband while working at a supermarket. He was white; there were some oriental guys who might have been interested in me, but he was so tall and so nice looking. We had a good chance to get to know each other because we worked together. Before I knew it, we were in love, we began living together and eventually we got married.

Stereotypes and Images

As with all minority groups, one of the most important factors in Korean adaptation is the attitudes, behaviors and feelings of the majority group. The balance of power is in the hands of the dominant group so that it is their laws, their perceptions, and their prescriptions which have long lasting effects on the minority in housing, education, employment, and opportunities for social interaction.

One function of prejudice, stereotypes, and images is that of avoidance so that even when different individuals are placed together in work, school, or social situations, prejudices, and negative stereotypes limit intimate interaction.

Historically, the Koreans suffered through the same negative Asian stereotypes that were a part of the Chinese and Japanese experience. Americans have had and continue to have difficulty in separating the various Asian groups ("they all look alike") so that initial contact between a white and a Korean is likely to be of a more generalized Asian image. The current Asian female stereotype is that they make good wives. The definition of "good" may include everything from being obedient, to taking care of the husband to not talking back, but as one white husband married to a Korean told us:

> Well first, she looked very good to me. Better than any of the white girls I knew. Then I knew that she wouldn't fool around and go out with other men. Then of course, we fell in love. My parents were somewhat reluctant about our getting married. They still remembered World War II and finally said it's okay as long as she wasn't Japanese.

Summary

The rates of in and outmarriages are related to the different Korean immigrant groups. The early immigrant group was small in number; they desired to become American desperately; they were cut off and isolated from their home country; they were scattered in a racially tolerant climate and acculturated rapidly. Their children achieved middle-class status; they ignored their bi-cultural heritage and when it came to getting married, generally chose non-Korean spouses.

The current group has developed a large, cohesive community; has maintained social networks that provide ample opportunities for in-group contact; have large proportions speaking the native tongue and maintaining old world values and therefore, when choosing spouses, prefer inmarriages.

It is clear that the Koreans are not a homogeneous group, and that the two groups mentioned are culturally, socially, and historically different; further, they entered the United States at different times and faced different conditions. It will be interesting to follow the development of the new immigrants and their children to see if there are predictable patterns in overall adaptation, so that with acculturation and the coming of new generations there will be a change in their marital patterns.

BIBLIOGRAPHY

Cha, Marn J. "Political Orientation of Koreans in Los Angeles," in Hyung-chan Kim (ed.), *The Korean Diaspora.* Santa Barbara, CA: The Clio Press, 1977, 191-203.

Harvey, Young Sook Kim, and Soon-Hyung Chung. *"The Koreans"* in John McDermott, Wen-Shing Tseng and Thomas Maretzki (eds.), *People and Cultures of Hawaii.* Honolulu: Univ. of Hawaii Press, 1980 pp. 135-154.

Hurh, Won Moo. "Comparative Study of Korean Immigrants in the United States: A Typology," in *Koreans in America.* Memphis Korea Christian Journal, 1977.

Kikumura, Akemi, and Harry H. Kitano. "Interracial Marriage: A Picture of the Japanese Americans." *Journal of Social Issues,* 1973 29, 2 67-81.

Kim, Bok-Lim. The Korean Child at School and Home, Project Report: U.S. Department of Health, Education and Welfare, 1980.

Kim, Bok-Lim. "An Appraisal of Korean Immigrant Service Needs," *Social Casework,* March 1976, 57, 139-148.

Kim, Bok-Lim C., and Margaret E. Condon. "A story of Asian Americans in Chicago: Their Socio-Economic Characteristics, Problems and Service Needs," Washington, D.C.: Interim Report to the Nation Institute of Mental Health, Department of Health, Education and Welfare, 1975.

Kim, Hyung-chan. "Koreans" in S. Thernstrom, A. Orlov and O. Handlin (eds.), *Harvard Encyclopedia of American Ethnic Groups.* Cambridge: Harvard University Press, 1980, 601-606.

Kim, Hyng-chan. "Koreans Community Organizations in America: Their Characteristics and Problems," in *The Korean Diaspora.* Santa Barbara, CA: Clio Press, 1977 65-83 (see Cha).

Kim, Hyung-chan. "Some Aspects of Social Demography of Korean Americans," in *The Korean Diaspora.* Santa Barbara, CA: Clio Press, 1977 109-112 (see Cha).

Kim, Hyung-chan. "Ethnic Enterprises Among Korean Immigrants in America," in *The Korean Diaspora.* Santa Barbara, CA: Clio Press, 1977 85-107 (see Cha).

Sherman, Diana. "Korea Town's Extent, Population Grows Daily," *Los Angeles Times,* February 25, 1979, Section VIII.

Ratliff, Bascom, Moon, Harriet F., and Gwendolyn Bonacci. "Intercultural Marriage: The Korean-American Experience," *Social Casework,* April 1978, 59, (4), 221-226.

INTERMARRIAGE OF MEXICAN AMERICANS

Edward Murguia
Ralph B. Cazares

Introduction

Early theoretical works on intermarriage by Davis (1941) and Merton (1941) have viewed intermarriage as mechanism indicating maintenance and/or change of ethnic boundaries. Bogardus (1933, 1958, 1968) included the concept of intermarriage in his index of social distance, a measure of the degree of acceptability of a particular minority by others, and Gordon (1964) identified intermarriage as a critical stage in a process of assimilation.

Thus, studies of Chicano intermarriage are important in understanding patterns of Chicano inclusion into (or exclusion from) American society. The degree of social control and institutionalized discrimination is a function of existing relationships between the majority and a minority. An increase in the number of primary relations (indicated by intermarriage) between these groups signals a dissolution of discriminatory and subordinating practices and less incumbered entrance of the minority group into the social institutions of the majority group (Gordon, 1964). On the other hand, intermarriage may indicate a weakening of ethnic cohesion and a loss of a highly valued ethnic culture (Murguia, 1982).

In this study, we propose to look at the intermarriage patterns of the Mexican American population in the United States. Rates of intermarriage in various places and time periods will be considered first. Next, factors related to Chicano exogamous behavior will be examined. These include the variables of social class, generation, group size and military status. The effect of the variable sex will then be discussed in greater detail as will the possible impact of outmarriage on the offspring of such a union.

Edward Murguia, Ph.D., is affiliated with the Department of Sociology, Trinity University. Ralph B. Cazares is a Graduate Student, Department of Sociology, Washington State University. Address all communications to: Edward Murguia, Department of Sociology, Trinity University, San Antonio, TX 78284. The authors would like to thank William R. Catton, Marilyn Ihinger-Tallman, Viktor Gecas, and Joe DeMartini for their perceptive comments on an earlier draft of this paper. We would also like to thank Dorothy Howell for her most competent secretarial assistance.

Rates of Chicano Intermarriage

A summary of rates of Chicano intermarriage is presented in Tables 1 and 2. In Table 1, data are summarized for studies conducted in three Texas counties (Bradshaw, 1960; Bean and Bradshaw, 1970; Alvirez and Bean, 1976; and Murguia and

Table 1

Summary of Studies of Chicano Intermarriage

Researcher	Area	Period	Percentage of Exogamous Individuals	Percentage of Exogamous Marriages
	Texas			
Bean and Bradshaw	San Antonio (Bexar Co.)	1850	5	10
Bean and Bradshaw	San Antonio (Bexar Co.)	1860	5	10
Bradshaw	San Antonio (Bexar Co.)	1940-55	10	17
Bean and Bradshaw	San Antonio (Bexar Co.)	1960	11	20
Murguia and Frisbie	San Antonio (Bexar Co.)	1964	14	24
Murguia and Frisbie	San Antonio (Bexar Co.)	1967	13	23
Murguia and Frisbie	San Antonio (Bexar Co.)	1971	14	24
Murguia and Frisbie	San Antonio (Bexar Co.)	1973	16	27
Alvirez and Bean	Corpus Christi (Nueces Co.)	1960-61	8	15
Alvirez and Bean	Corpus Christi (Nueces Co.)	1970-71	9	16
Alvirez and Bean	Edinburg (Hidalgo Co.)	1961	3	5
Alvirez and Bean	Edinburg (Hidalgo Co.)	1971	5	9
	New Mexico			
Cochrane	Las Cruces (Dona Ana Co.)	1915	0	0
Holscher, et al.	Las Cruces (Dona Ana Co.)	1953	10	18
Holscher, et al.	Las Cruces (Dona Ana Co.)	1967	11	20
Holscher, et al.	Las Cruces (Dona Ana Co.)	1977	15	27
Johnson	Albuquerque (Bernalillo Co.)	1915-16	8	14
Zeleny	Albuquerque (Bernalillo Co.)	1924-40	8	15
Johnson	Albuquerque (Bernalillo Co.)	1945-46	12	22
Gonzalez	Albuquerque (Bernalillo Co.)	1953	13	23
Gonzalez	Albuquerque (Bernalillo Co.)	1964	19	33
Murguia and Frisbie	Albuquerque (Bernalillo Co.)	1967	31	48
Murguia and Frisbie	Albuquerque (Bernalillo Co.)	1971	24	39
Holscher, et al.	Seven Counties[*]	1953	9	16
Holscher, et al.	Seven Counties[*]	1967	12	22
Holscher, et al.	Seven Counties[*]	1977	14	24
	Arizona			
Stone, et al.	Nogales (Santa Cruz Co.)	1952-62	9	17
	California			
Panunzio	Los Angeles (Los Angeles Co.)	1924-33	9	17
Grebler, et al.	Los Angeles (Los Angeles Co.)	1963	25	40
Schoen, et al.	California[**]	1962	38	55
Schoen, et al.	California[**]	1966	37	54
Schoen, et al.	California[**]	1970	36	53
Schoen, et al.	California[**]	1974	34	51
Burma, et al.	San Bernadino (San Bernadino Co.)	1970-77	34	51

[*]The seven New Mexican county seats and counties are: Las Cruces (Cona Ana Co.), Roswell(Chavez Co.), Carrizozo(Lincoln Co.), Deming(Luna Co.) Las Vegas (San Miguel Co.) Socorro(Socorro Co.), and Taos(Taos Co.). The rates in this table are the combined rates for all seven counties. Rates for each county for 1953, 1967, and 1977 can be found in Holscher, et al., (1979).
[**]The Schoen, et al., 1978) data include the entire state.

Sources: Data adapted from Bean and Bradshaw, 1970 (San Antonio, 1850, 1860, 1960); Bradshaw, 1960 (San Antonio, 1940-55); Murguia and Frisbie, 1977 (San Antonio, 1964, 1967, 1971, 1973; Albuquerque, 1967, 1971); Alvirez and Bean, 1976 (Corpus Christi, 1960-61, 1970-71; Edinburgh, 1961, 1971) Gonzalez, 1969 (Las Cruces, 1915; Albuquerque, 1915-16, 1945-46, 1953, 1964); Holscher, et al., 1979 (Las Cruces, 1953, 1967, 1977; Seven counties, 1953, 1967, 1977; San Bernadino, 1970-1977); Stone, et al., 1963 (Nogales, 1952-62); Grebler, et al., 1970 (Albuquerque, 1924-40; Los Angeles, 1924-33, 1963); Schoen, et al., 1978 (California, 1962, 1966, 1970, 1974).

Frisbie, 1977), for eight counties in New Mexico (Gonzalez, 1969; Murguia and Frisbie, 1977; and Holscher et al., 1979), for one county in Arizona (Stone et al., 1963); for two California counties (Panunzio, 1942; Grebler et al., 1970; Burma et al., 1979), and for the entire state of California (Schoen et al., 1978). The data are presented as percentages of exogamous individuals and percentages of exogamous marriages (Rodman, 1965). The individual rate of exogamy is the number of inter-marriages divided by the total number of marriages (both endogamous and ex-ogmaous) involving minority persons.

Texas. The summary of studies of Texas counties indicates a gradual increase in exogamy over time. While only five percent of Chicanos in San Antonio were exogamous in 1860, the percentage has increased, but slowly, reaching 16 percent in 1973. Studies in Nueces and Hidalgo counties in 1961 and 1971 by Alvirez and Bean (1976) show a similar pattern of slow increase over a much briefer (ten year) time span.

New Mexico. The New Mexico summarized data show exogamy patterns similar to those of Texas. Again, there is a general increase in individual and marriage ex-ogamous rates over time. Bennalillo County (Albuquerque) has been the focus of most intermarriage studies conducted in the state; the data for this county show a low exogamy rate for individuals of 8 percent and 14 percent for exogamous mar-riages in 1916, and a high of 31 and 48 percent individual and marriage exogamy rates, respectively, for 1967. However, both rates decrease (to 24 and 39 percent) in 1971.

Arizona. Intermarriage rates in Nogales, a border town, are considerably higher than the rates for the Texas border towns in Hidalgo County. The rates resemble those of Las Cruces (Dona Ana County) New Mexico, for a similar time period. Clearly, more study of this state and particularly of the large urban areas of Phoenix and Tucson would be valuable.

California. The California summary data reveal a much higher exogamy rate for that state as compared to Texas and New Mexico. When the 1963 Los Angeles County data are compared with the 1964 Bexar County and 1964 Bernalillo County data (the closest comparable time period available), the California individual exogamy rate of 25 percent is considerably higher than that of the other two counties (14 and 19 percent respectively). Schoen et al. (1978) notes an even higher rate of 38 percent for all of California during the same time period. They also show that for the entire state there has been a steady but not very great decrease in the amount of exogamy from 1962 to 1974. The Burma et al. (1979) data indicate that intermarriage rates in San Bernardino County parallel statewide exogamy rates.

Table 2 presents cumulative rates of intermarriage for Chicanos in the United States by sex and age for 1970, derived from census data. Rates for younger age groups are higher than for older age groups, indicating an assimilative trend, and the total percentage is slightly higher for females than for males. Overall, approx-imately 16 percent of the Chicano married population is married exogamously. In general, then, we see a trend toward increasing rates of outmarriage with each new age group.

However, county intermarriage data indicate that in areas where outmarriage rates

Table 2

Cumulative Rates of Intermarriage for Chicanos

in the United States by Sex and Age, 1970

Age	Percentage of Exogamous Males	Percentage of Exogamous Females
45 and over	12	13
25-44	17	17
16-24	23	21
Total, 16 and over	16	17

Source: A Study of Selected Socio-Economic Characteristics of Ethnic
         Minorities, Based on the 1970 Census, Volume 1: Americans of
         Spanish Origin, U.S. Department of Health, Education and Welfare,
         p. 45.

have been relatively high, (California, Bernalillo County) there seems to be a leveling of or even a decrease in rates of exogamy. In areas where rates have been relatively low (e.g., Nueces County, Hidalgo County, Dona Ana County), continuing increases in exogamy have been recorded. Consequently, although rates have varied considerably in the different areas researched, a convergence of rates between those locations with high exogamy rates and those with low rates seem to be occurring at this time.

A possible reason for this is that areas where rates of outmarriage have been high because of their relatively greater ethnic tolerance and economic opportunities have tended to be attractive to first generation individuals whose rates of outmarriage are low. Also these areas were centers of minority ethnic consciousness during the 1960s and 1970s. Areas where rates of exogamy were very low, on the other hand, had begun to be affected by the results of civil rights legislation and by the relatively liberal national mass media, and ethnic barriers could not be maintained as rigidly as they had been in the past.

Variables Related to Exogamy

Several variables related to Chicano outmarriage have been identified in the Chicano intermarriage literature. In this section, we will examine some of these variables—social class, generation, group size and military status—and their relationship to Chicano exogamy.

Social class. According to Merton (1941:367) most marriages occur "within a social class, if only for reasons of mutual accessibility and participation in common social groups by members of the same class but the norm is sufficiently flexible to allow frequent interclass unions." Initial contact between Anglo Americans and those of Mexican descent in the 1800s reflected great class differences. Anglo American settlers with largely middle class traits did not find an equivalently large Mexican middle class in the conquered territories. McWilliams (1968:75) speculates that "if a large [Chicano] middle-class element had existed, the adjustment between the two cultures might have been facilitated and the amount of intermarriage might have been greater." Not unexpectedly, then, the earliest recorded Chicano intermarriage rates are not high (e.g., Bexar County, 1850).[1]

Approximately 100 years after the conquest of the Southwest, McDonagh (1949: 459) was still able to generalize that Mexican American status levels appear to be as follows: (1) their social status is in the lowest quartile, (2) officially they are listed as "white" but are still discriminated against, (3) their educational status is modest, and (4) their economic status is in the lowest quartile. Class differences in the 1940s (as currently) operate as barriers to increased rates of exogamy.

Upward mobility for Mexican Americans, as for other American ethnic and racial groups, is positively associated with intermarriage (Grebler et al., 1970). The higher the economic status of Chicano males, the greater the rate of exogamy. Additionally, exogamous Mexican American females tend to marry males of relatively high status.

Generation. Removal from immigrant status increases exogamy (Bossard, 1939; Grebler et al., 1970:409). Third generation Chicanos exhibit higher rates of exogamy than do those of the second generation, who, in turn, outmarry to a greater extent than those of the first generation. This finding holds for both males and females.

It follows then that continuing immigration from Mexico will have the effect of lowering outmarriage rates which otherwise would be expected continually to increase over time. (Incidentally, Chicano *endogamous* marriages tend to be "generationally endogamous" (Grebler et al., 1970:409). That is, individuals who marry endogamously tend to marry those of the same generation as themselves.)

Group size. The greater the absolute and relative size of a Mexican American population in an area the less outmarriage it exhibits. Holscher et al., (1979), for example, demonstrate that of the New Mexican counties they studied, those containing the highest percentages of Chicanos relative to the majority population had the lowest outmarriage rates.

Military status and wartime. Bradshaw (1960) documents increased rates of Chicano outmarriage for those periods of military buildup precipitated by the Second World War and the Korean War. He believed that wartime was conducive to exogamy "not only because of a large influx of military personnel but also because of a relaxing of norms governing exogamy" (Bradshaw, 1960:51). Murguia (1979) demonstrates that military status for Chicano males and possibly for Anglo males is positively related to intermarriage.

Differentials in Intermarriage by Sex

A universal finding in the study of Mexican American intermarriage is that Spanish surnamed females tend to marry outside of their ethnicity more frequently than do Spanish surnamed males. Thus, of the two types of intermarriages (Anglo male/Spanish surname female; Spanish surname male/Anglo female) the former type is the more prevalent.[2]

Using exchange theory, if we make some assumptions concerning societal attitudes toward phenotype and surnames, and assumptions concerning class and cultural differences between the majority and the minority, an explanation for the greater amount of outmarriage of Spanish surname females and for the possibly greater stability of these marriages can be developed.[3]

The assumptions are as follows:

1. In American society, a Caucasian phenotype is more highly valued than a Mongoloid (Native American) appearance (see Warner and Srole, 1945:286).
2. A Spanish surname is less acceptable than a non-Spanish (usually Northern European) surname.
3. Males marry down in class to a greater extent that do females. (Hollingshead, 1950; Roth and Peck, 1951).
4. Lower and working class individuals greatly aspire to middle class standing. Downward mobility is highly undesirable.
5. The Mexican American population is more heavily concentrated in the lower and working classes than is the majority (Anglo American) population.
6. The Mexican American population holds more traditional (less egalitarian) attitudes toward the role of women, both because of historical and religious factors, and because the population has proportionally greater numbers in the lower and working classes.

Given the above, four advantages[4] accrue to Spanish surname females on marrying Anglo males. They gain:

1. A Caucasian phenotype in both husband and, at least partially, in offspring.
2. A non-Spanish surname which is more acceptable in American society than a Spanish surname.
3. Often, an increase in social class standing (or, at least, no downward mobility).
4. Possibly, a greater egalitarianism on the part of majority males as compared to minority males.

The major advantage in intermarriage for Anglo males is that they marry women who are husband and family oriented,[5] so oriented because of their class standing as well as their cultural and religious socialization.

Turning to the second type of outmarriage, that involving Chicano males and Anglo females, there seem to be fewer advantages for either the minority and majority individuals involved. Chicano males do gain a phenotypic advantage in marrying Caucasian women.[6] However, to the extent that majority females tend not to be as husband and family oriented as minority males have come to expect,[7] family conflicts could arise. The majority female gains neither in phenotype, surname, nor possibly in egalitarianism.

For these reasons, greater stability is predicted for the Anglo male/Spanish surname female type of intermarriage as compared to the Spanish surname male/Anglo female type of marriage.

The Children of Intermarrieds

In general, there are three indicators by which an individual can be identified as a Chicano by others. The first is by having a non-Caucasian phenotype. The second is through the ability to speak Spanish (Speaking English with a Spanish accent, or even speaking no English at all indicates even less acculturation). The third is by possessing a Spanish name, primarily a Spanish surname (First and second given names in Spanish indicate that the possessor is less acculturated as well).

All of these indicators can be weakened through intermarriage. Children of intermarriages between Mexican Americans and Anglo Americans[8] will tend to look more Caucasian than offspring of two Chicano parents. Additionally, there is less likelihood of Spanish being spoken at home in an intermarried family than in an ethnically homogeneous Chicano family. However, because of the impact of the mass media and the schools, maintaining Spanish is difficult even in an ethnically homogeneous home. Finally, offspring of Anglo males and Mexican American females (the type of intermarriage which comprised more than half of all Chicano intermarriages) will not possess Spanish surnames at all.

The three indicators act upon the single most important determinant of ethnicity, namely, self identification in terms of an ethnic identity. Children of intermarriages will not be able to unequivocally to call themselves Chicanos. They might consider themselves as "part" or "half" Chicano or they might not identify themselves as Chicano at all.[9] Individuals not looked upon as ethnics by others may choose not to consider themselves ethnic, because self image is, in part, a reflection of what others see in us (Cooley, 1964:184).

We propose that the more Caucasian in phenotype the offspring the less likely the offspring will be considered by others, and, by themselves, as Chicano. Also, children of Anglo males and Mexican females, in not possessing a Spanish surname, will be less likely to be identified and to self identify as Chicano than children of Chicano males and Anglo females. Interestingly, though, because mothers spend more time with children during the critical early years of socialization than do fathers, we believe that children of Anglo males and Mexican American females, being raised by ethnic mothers who consciously or unconciously instill in their children ethnic traits, will be more likely to exhibit traits associated with the Mexican American culture than children of Chicano fathers and Anglo mothers.

A child born of an intermarriage may find it difficult to totally integrate into either parent's social group. However, what an individual loses in comfort and integration he may gain in insight and understanding of both groups. In addition, there may increasingly be enough others in his similar situation that he may lose his sense of uniqueness and isolation.

This marginal situation (Stonequist, 1937) becomes seriously uncomfortable only if the two groups are in conflict. For many children of Chicano/Anglo intermarriages, their dual ethnicity might not matter in most of their day-to-day existence, just as being part Irish or part Italian matters little.

In case of conflict, the minority is usually the more tolerant and accepting of marginal individuals. Also, marginal individuals are usually among the first to mediate and to attempt to achieve a compromise solution to conflict because when it erupts they, being caught in the middle, experience the most serious difficulties.

Conclusion

In this study, we have presented empirical evidence indicating the beginning of convergence of intermarriage rates in areas where previously there has been great divergence. In the long run, however, it is difficult to imagine anything but an overall slow increase in rates of Chicano intermarriage, as Chicanos in increasing numbers reach middle class status. This population, as a whole, is not geographically isolated as are some Native American tribes, nor does it have its own parallel economic, educational, nor even religious institutions. As this population moves out of ethnic enclaves (barrios), it moves in the direction of increasing contact on an equal basis with the majority population on the job, in church, and at school.

On the other hand, there are three factors which for the foreseeable future we feel will keep the Chicano population from complete absorption into the majority society. First is that the group is, in part, non-Caucasian and therefore physically distinct from and identifiable by the majority. It has been long noted that racial differences are among the strongest barriers to the development of primary relationships and subsequent intermarriage between groups.

Second, there is the continuing immigration of both documented and undocumented workers from Mexico to the United States. First generation Chicanos have a lower rate of outmarriage than do subsequent generations of Mexican Americans. Finally, the close proximity to Mexico provides continuing contact and continuous movement back and forth across the border; this has the effect of limiting absorption through intermarriage.

In the future, it is predicted that the Chicano population will continue to exhibit an even greater diversity than at present. First generation immigrants will be attempting to learn the language and some of the customs of the country to which they come for economic reasons, while some of the more affluent and established (third generation and beyond) of this population will be struggling to teach their children the importance of learning Spanish and of the maintenance of their cultural heritage. It is among these latter population segments that intermarriage is most likely to take place.

NOTES

1. Of course, vast cultural differences separated the two groups as well at this time, greatly affecting the amount of intermarriage.
2. Although the differentials are not large.
3. This hypothesis has yet to be subjected to an empirical investigation, however.
4. These advantages, of course, are often unconscious and unstated. Clearly, an individual rarely consciously calculates the advantages presented here.
5. On asking Mexican American women as to differences they perceived between themselves and their non-ethnic counterparts, the concepts of their being more "understanding" than Anglo females came through. The term "understanding" could be interpreted as subordination,

however. It must be emphasized that these interviews were preliminary and exploratory in nature and that additional research is required for more conclusive findings in this area.

6. The attraction of white women to minority males has been the subject of much introspection (see Fanon, 1968:63–82; Malcolm X, 1966:66–88, 93–96, 135–36; Cleaver, 1970:17–29). One social psychological interpretation has it that in gaining the affection of ("conquering") a white woman, the minority male symbolically attacks and conquers the majority society which has oppressed him.

7. This is particularly true of upwardly mobile Chicano males from working class backgrounds.

8. By far the greatest amount of Chicano intermarriages occurs between Chicanos and whites (as opposed to non-whites). (Burma, 1963).

9. Once upon asking an individual as to whether she was a Chicana or not, she replied, "I'm not, but my mother is." Her mother was a Mexican American from San Antonio, Texas, and her father was a German from Germany who had come to the United States in some military capacity and had met the girl's mother in San Antonio. The girl had a clearly Caucasian phenotype.

REFERENCES

Alvirez, David, and Frank D. Bean. "The Mexican American family." In C.H. Mindel and R.W. Habenstein (eds.), *Ethnic Families in America*. New York: Elsevier, 1976, 271–292.

Barron, Milton L. "Research on intermarriage: A survey of accomplishments and prospects." *American Journal of Sociology*, 1951, *57*:249–255.

Bean, Frank D., and Benjamin S. Bradshaw. "Intermarriage between persons of Spanish and non-Spanish surname: Changes from the mid-19th to the mid-20th century." *Social Science Quarterly*, 1970, *51*:389–395.

Bogardus, Emory S. "A social distance scale." *Sociology and Social Research*, 1933, *17*:265–271.

Bogardus, Emory S. "Racial distance changes in the United States during the past thirty years." *Sociology and Social Research*, 1958, *43*:127–135.

Bogardus, Emory S. "Comparing racial distance in Ethiopia, South Africa, and the United States." *Sociology and Social Research*, 1968, *52*:149–156.

Bossard, James H.S. "Nationality and nativity as factors in marriage." *American Sociological Review*, 1939, *4*:792–798.

Bradshaw, Benjamin S. "Some demographic aspects of marriage: A comparative study of three ethnic groups." Masters thesis, University of Texas at Austin, 1960.

Bugelski, B.R. "Assimilation through intermarriage." *Social Forces*, 1961, *40*:148–153.

Burma, John H. "Interethnic marriage in Los Angeles, 1948–1959." *Social Forces*, 1963, *42*(2):156–165.

Burma, John H., Gary A. Cretser, and Joseph J. Leon. "Confidential and non-confidential marriage: A study of Spanish surnamed marriages in San Bernardino County, California, 1970–1977." *Marriage and Family Counselors Quarterly*, 1979, *13*:2.

Cleaver, Eldridge. *Soul on Ice*. New York: Dell, 1970.

Cooley, Charles Horton. *Human Nature and the Social Order*. New York: Schocken, 1964.

Cretser, Gary A., and Joseph J. Leon. "Intermarriage in the U.S.: The last fifty years." Paper presented at the annual meeting of the Pacific Sociological Association, Anaheim, 1979.

Crull, Sue R., and Brent, T.B. "Bogardus social distance in the 1970's." *Sociology and Social Research*, 1979, *63*:771–783.

Davis, Kingsley. "Intermarriage in caste societies." *American Anthropologist*, 1941, *43*:376–395.

Fanon, Frantz. *Black Skin, White Masks*. New York: Grove Press, 1968.

Gonzalez, Nancie L. *The Spanish-Americans of New Mexico: A Heritage of Pride*. Albuquerque: The University of New Mexico Press, 1969.

Gordon, Milton M. *Assimilation in American Life*. New York: Oxford University Press, 1964.

Grebler, Leo, Joan W. Moore, and Ralph C. Guzman. *The Mexican-American People: The Nation's Second Largest Minority*. New York: The Free Press, 1970.

Hollingshead, August B. "Cultural factors in the selection of marriage mates." *American Sociological Review*, 1950, *15*:619–627.

Holscher, Louis, Charles Varni, and Letty Naranjo. "Chicano exogamous marriages in New Mexico." Paper presented at the annual meeting of the Pacific Sociological Association, Anaheim, 1979.

Malcolm X. *The Autobiography of Malcolm X*. New York: Grove Press, 1966.

McDonagh, Edward C. "Status levels of Mexicans." *Sociology and Social Research*, 1949, *33*:449–459.

Merton, Robert K. "Intermarriage and social structure: fact and theory." *Psychiatry*, 1941, *4*:361–374.

McWilliams, Carey. *North From Mexico*. New York: Greenwood Press, 1968.

Mittelbach, Frank G., Joan W. Moore, and Ronald McDaniel. "Intermarriage of Mexican-Americans, advanced report 6." Los Angeles: Graduate School of Business Administration, The University of California at Los Angeles, 1966.

Mittelbach, Frank G., and Joan W. Moore. "Ethnic endogamy—the case of Mexican Americans." *American Journal of Sociology*, 1968, *74*:50–62.

Murguia, Edward. *Assimilation, Colonialism and the Mexican American People*. Austin: Center for Mexican American Studies, The University of Texas at Austin, 1975.

Murguia, Edward, and W. Parker Frisbie. "Trends in Mexican American intermarriage: Recent findings in perspective." *Social Science Quarterly*, 1977, *58*:374–389.

Murguia, Edward. *Chicano Intermarriage*. San Antonio: Trinity University Press, 1982.

Murguia, Edward. "Military status and Chicano intermarriage." Paper presented at the annual meeting of the American Sociological Association, Boston, 1979.

Panunzio, Constantine. "Intermarriage in Los Angeles, 1924–33." *American Journal of Sociology*, 1942, *47*(5):690–701.

Rodman, Hyman. "Technical note on two rates of mixed marriage." *American Sociological Review*, 1965, *30*:776–778.

Roth, Julius, and Robert F. Peck. "Social class and social mobility factors related to marital adjustment." *American Sociological Review*, 1951, *16*:478–487.

Schoen, Robert, Verne E. Nelson, and Marion Collins. "Intermarriage among Spanish surnamed Californians, 1962–1974." *International Migration Review*, 1978, *12*(3):359–369.

Stone, Robert C., Frank A. Petroni, and Thomas J. McCleneghan. "Nogales, Arizona: An overview of economic and interethnic patterns in a border community." *Arizona Review of Business and Public Research*, 1963, *12*:4–29.

Stonequist, Everett V. *The Marginal Man*. New York: Scribner, 1937.

U.S. Department of Health, Education and Welfare. A study of selected socio-economic characteristics of ethnic minorities, based on the 1970 census, volume 1: Americans of Spanish origin. Washington, D.C.: U.S. Government Printing Office, 1974.

Warner, W. Lloyd, and Leo Srole. *The Social Systems of American Ethnic Groups*. New Haven: Yale University Press, 1945.

GUIDE TO REFERENCE SOURCES
FOR INTERMARRIAGE

Laura A. Shepard
Jonathan B. Jeffery

This section of *Marriage and Family Review* is the second in a series of reference sources pertaining to the theme of each issue. A reader seeking more information on intermarriage may utilize the following bibliography to review the literature. To keep apprised of the latest literature on the topic, two recommended means are a combination of scanning current sources (e.g., annuals, trade catalogs) and computer searching of available data bases. An explanation of computerized literature searching can be found in the last issue, Volume 4, issues 3/4.

The types of sources included in this bibliography are encyclopedias, subject bibliographies, indexes and abstracts, and annual bibliographies. Definitions and special notes will be given here to assist the reader in selecting the most desirable sources for the research. The most general sources, books and encyclopedias, are included to give the reader background on the topic of intermarriage and locate other bibliographies normally given in these sources. A book that is excellent for background material is *Interracial Marriage: Expectations and Realities* by Irving R. Stuart and Lawrence Edwin Abt. It includes information on interracial marriage in various cultures along with bibliographic notes. The annual bibliographies can provide retrospective and current surveys of the literature. Subject bibliographies, as the name suggests, are limited to one subject. As a consequence, the ones provided here may form a basic core of information on interracial marriage. Indexes generally analyze books, periodicals, or other publications. All the indexes and most of the reference sources given in this bibliography will be accompanied by possible access terms to locate information on intermarriage.

Encyclopedias

Encyclopedia Judaica. Jerusalem, Encyclopaedia Judaica; New York, Macmillan, 1972.
　　See: "Mixed Marriage, intermarriage"
Harvard Encyclopedia of American Ethnic Groups. Stephan Thernstron, ed. Cambridge, Mass., Harvard University Press, 1980.
　　See: "Intermarriage"

Laura A. Shepard and Jonathan B. Jeffery are Associate Librarians in the Reference Department, University of Delaware Library.

International Encyclopedia of the Social Sciences. David L. Sills, ed. New York, Macmillan Co. and The Free Press, 1968.
  See: "Intermarriage" under chapter on "Assimilation"
New Catholic Encyclopedia. New York, McGraw-Hill Book Co., 1967.
  See: "Mixed religion (impediment to marriage)"

Subject Bibliographies

Cashman, Marc, and Barry Klein, eds. *Bibliography of American Ethnology*. Rye, NY, Todd Publications, 1976.
  See: "Miscegenation"
Goode, William J., Elizabeth Hopkins, Helen M. McClure. *Social Systems and Family Patterns: A Propositional Inventory*. New York, Bobbs-Merrill, 1971.
  Using a dictionary approach, this work lists "research findings" on the family. There are several subdivisions (i.e., clan, ethnic, racial) under the heading "Intermarriage."
Miller, Elizabeth, comp. *The Negro in America: A Bibliography*. Second edition compiled and revised by Mary L. Fisher. Cambridge, Mass., Harvard University Press, 1970.
  See: "Intermarriage and interracial adoption"
Mogey, John M. *Sociology of Marriage and Family Behavior, 1957-1968*. The Hague, Mouton, 1971.
  International in scope, this bibliography includes materials on all levels of intermarriage. *See*: Section 406, "Marriage and divorce-intermarriage: religious, class, ethnic, caste."
Myers, Hector F., Phyllis G. Rana, Marcia Harris, comps. *Black Child Development in America, 1927-1977*. Westport, Conn., Greenwood Press, 1979.
  This bibliography includes information on the children of black-white marriages.
Obudho, Constance E. *Black-White Racial Attitudes: An Annotated Bibliography*. Westport, Conn., Greenwood Press, 1976.
  Although this only includes one citation under "Interracial marriage," it has numerous other headings that will include related material.
West, Earle H., comp. *A Bibliography of Doctoral Research on the Negro, 1933-1966*. Ann Arbor, MI, Xerox University Microfilms, 1969. Supplemented by *A Bibliography of Doctoral Research on the Negro, 1967-1977* by Joan B. Peebles, 1978.
  See: "Marriage, family, child rearing"
Work, Monroe N., comp. *A Bibliography of the Negro in Africa and America*. New York, H.W. Wilson, 1928; Reprinted New York, Octagon, 1967.
  See: Section 38, "Race mixture"

Indexing and Abstracting Sources

America: History and Life. Santa Barbara, CA, Clio Press, 1964-Quarterly.

See: "Intermarriage, "Marriage, interracial," "Marriage, mixed," "Miscegenation"

Comprehensive Dissertation Index. Ann Arbor, MI, Xerox University Microfilms, 1973. Has annual supplements.

Indexes *Dissertation Abstracts International. See*: Keywords "Intermarriage" and "Marriage" under main headings Social Sciences, Psychology, and Education.

Cumulative Book Index: A World List of Books in the English Language. New York, Wilson, 1933– .

See: "Interracial marriage," "Marriage, mixed"

Dissertation Abstracts International. Ann Arbor, MI, University Microfilms, 1938– . Monthly.

See: The same keywords as *Comprehensive Dissertation Index*.

Gallup, George H. *The Gallup Poll: Public Opinion, 1935–1971*. New York, Random House. 1972. Supplemented with cumulations by Scholarly Resources, Wilmington, DE.

Reports data from polls of American political and social opinion. *See*: "Religion-mixed marriages," "Interfaith marriages," "Interracial marriages"

Index to Legal Periodicals. New York, Wilson, 1980– . Monthly.

See: "Miscegenation" for articles and court cases.

Index to Periodical Articles By and About Blacks (formerly *Index to Selected Negro Periodicals*, then *Index to Periodical Articles By and About Negroes*). Boston, G.K. Hall, 1950– . Annual.

See: "Intermarriage," "Marriages, interracial," "Miscegenation"

Indexing and Abstracting Sources

Inventory of Marriage and Family Literature. Minneapolis, MI, Minnesota Family Study Center and the Institute of Life Insurance, 1967– .

See: "Interethnic," "Intermarriage," "Interfaith," "Mixed marriage," "Marriage," "Exogamous," "Exogamy"

New York Times Index. New York, Times, 1851– . Semimonthly.

See: "Marriages"

Psychological Abstracts. Lancaster, PA, American Psychological Association, 1927– . Monthly.

See: "Exogamous marriage," "Interfaith marriage," "Interracial marriage"

Readers' Guide to Periodical Literature. New York, Wilson, 1905– . Semimonthly.

Subject headings vary over the years. For earlier years, see "Intermarriage of races," "Marriages, mixed," "Miscegenation." More recent headings are "Interracial marriage" and "Marriage, mixed."

Religion Index One: Periodicals (formerly *Index to Religious Periodical Literature*). Chicago, American Theological Library Association, 1949– .

See: "Intermarriage," "Marriage, mixed"

Social Sciences Citation Index. Philadelphia, Institute for Scientific Information, 1969–   . Published three times a year.

    Sample permuterm keyword subject index terms: "Interracial," "Intermarriage," "Intercultural," "Interethnic," "Miscegenation," "Marriage"

Social Sciences Index. New York, Wilson, 1974–   . Quarterly.

    See: "Endogamy and exogamy," "Marriage, mixed," "Interracial marriage," "Intermarriage of races"

Sociological Abstracts. New York, Sociological Abstracts, 1952–   . Published six times a year.

    See: "Intermarriage," "Marriage"

Annual Bibliographies

American Statistics Index. Washington, Congressional Information Service, 1973–   . Annual, with monthly supplements.

    See: "Marriage" for Bureau of the Census statistics on intermarriage.

Bibliographic Index; A cumulative bibliography of bibliographies. New York, Wilson, 1938–   .

    See: "Interracial marriage," "Endogamy and exogamy"

International Bibliography of the Social Sciences: International Bibliography of Sociology. London, Tavistock Publications; Chicago, Aldine, 1952–   . Annual.

    See: "Mixed marriage," "Endogamy"

Schomburg Center for Research and Black Culture. *Bibliographic Guide to Black Studies*. Boston, G.K. Hall, 1975–   . Annual.

    See: "Miscegenation," "Intermarriage"

Subject Guide to Books in Print: An Index to the Publishers' Trade List Annual. New York, Bowker, 1957–   . Annual.

    See: "Interracial marriage"

ANALYTIC ESSAY:
INTERCULTURAL AND INTERRACIAL MARRIAGE

Kris Jeter

The subject of marriage has enjoyed popularity throughout the history of the written word. Surprisingly, however, books on intercultural and interracial marriage are sparse. Traditional professional literature on the family tends to identify "intermarriage" as interreligious marriage and to speak about intermarriage with pessimism. Recent books on marriage and the family for clinicians, lay people, and researchers are particularly few in number. This could be because there has been no systematic, large-scale studies on which to base a book.

A look at authors, themselves, could provide insight on this information lag. Many authors and researchers develop interest in a subject because of their personal involvement. Thus, one assumption could be that authors and researchers are not themselves members of intercultural marriages. Authors and researchers must love their topic to become immersed in the subject and to expend large amounts of energy and time. The authors of the works discussed in this essay agree that there is a lack of interest and even indifference among social scientists about intercultural marriage. Most authors seek to avoid criticism and negative emotional expressions which could happen no matter how gingerly they approach this potentially explosive subject. Still, I predict that this topic will be increasingly in vogue in the near future.

This analytical essay examines the motives for intercultural marriage. Primary reference is made to four books which represent a cross section of cultural, historical, sociological, and psychological perspectives of intermarriage. They are discussed in the following order:

Bernard, Richard M. *The Melting Pot and the Altar: Marital Assimilation in Early Twentieth-Century Wisconsin.* Minneapolis, Minnesota: University of Minnesota Press, 1980.

Conner, John W. *A Study of the Marital Stability of Japanese War Brides.* San Francisco, California: R and E Research Associates, 1976.

Kris Jeter, PhD, is a Trainer, Human Development Specialist and Associate with Beacon Research Associates, Ltd., Inc.

Porterfield, Ernest. *Black and White Mixed Marriages*. Chicago, Illinois: Nelson-Hall, 1978.

Tseng, Wen-Shing; John F. McDermott, Jr.; and Thomas W. Maretzki, Editors. *Adjustment in Intercultural Marriage*. Honolulu, Hawaii: The University Press of Hawaii, 1977.

European Immigrants

Historian, Richard M. Bernard's primary objective in *The Melting Pot* is to discover the patterns and rates of marital assimilation and factors promoting inter-marriages among three major groups of people living in Wisconsin. The period covered is from statehood in 1848 to the passage of the National Immigration Act in 1921. Colonial native-stock settled first in Wisconsin. Between 1870 and 1910 native stock comprised 30% of Wisconsin's population and 70% were foreign-born or first- and second-generation immigrants. The second group are the later arrivals, Eastern European immigrants from Austria, Bohemia, Poland, and Russia. State marriage registrations and federal census data are used to determine intermarriage rates.

First, Bernard reviews the last fifty years of sociological theories on intermarriage. Despite the diverseness of the samples and settings, he isolates two major causes of intermarriage: the individual's social characteristics and relationships with other marriageable persons. Bernard develops a composite model of eight characteristics of people who out-marry. These are English- and German-speaking background, higher social class, mixed parentage, older age, previous marriage, Protestant country origin, residence in a small community, and second-generation status. This model is tested using stepwise multiple regression analysis.

The model is effective for studying Eastern European immigrants but ineffective for Western Europeans. One interpretation of this situation is that mid-twentieth century sociological theories were written by contemporaries and even representatives of the later arriving Eastern European immigrants. Hence, the selection of the variables for the model. Two characteristics which significantly promoted intercultural marriages among Eastern Europeans are mixed parentage and second-generation status.

After examining the state and federal data based, Bernard concludes the exogamy or out-group marriage by members of any of the studied groups was prevalent and tended to be related to geographic availability and social similarity. Marital assimilation of most first-generation immigrants meant intermarriage with native stock and not with foreign-born people. In 1880, the Eastern European immigrants' exogamy figures for the first-generation were 21.0% and 30.8% for second-generation. Thirty years later, in 1910, the Western European immigrants outmarried at the rates of 34.5% from the first-generation and 46.6% for the second-generation. In contrast, the exogamy data for the Eastern European immigrants who had arrived more recently than the Western European immigrants were for the first-generation 17.5% and for the second-generation 40.5%. State and federal data indicate that Western European immigrants outmarried more than those from Eastern Europe because of their comparatively larger second-generation population, earlier arrival to the United States, and rural residence.

Japanese War Brides

Sociologist, John W. Conner, conducted research in the 1960s on 25 marriages of American Caucasian males and native-born Japanese females married between 1950 and 1958 to determine the marital stability and relevance of culture, race, and religion factors. A 32 item open-ended questionnaire, "The Marital Adjustment Form," was the basis of a two-hour interview conducted with each couple. An American Caucasian sample was utilized for comparison purposes.

Conner had difficulty in obtaining the intercultural sample. He obtained couples by chance, through personal contact, checking the parentage of Eurasian children, and searching through the Sacramento, California telephone directory for Japanese women with European surnames. The independent nature, even stubborn quality, of the partners surfaced, not only in recruiting study participants, but in the answers to the questionnaire.

The intercultural couples were married after World War II and the earlier the date of their marriage, the more military red tape, official disapproval, and nonacceptance by family and friends occurred. Families of both the husband and wife were either apathetic or against the marriage. These negatives were discounted by the couples because the in-laws' residence was out-of-state or out-of-country. Five intercultural couples Conner interviewed were divorced. He observed that all five of the divorced husbands exhibited passive and submissive personalities. Thus, Conner proposes that adjusted intercultural marriage partners tend to be marginal individuals with no strong family ties or institutional loyalties who survive through assertive, even aggressive and defensive actions.

Marriages between Blacks and Whites

Sociologist, Ernest Porterfield, writes "a systematic ethnographic description of 40 black-white families." Interactions between family members, kin, and society are examined. Porterfield highlights the potentiality and difficulties in forming through interracial marriage "an egalitarian multiracial society."

Porterfield first presents a historical perspective of black-white families. Indentured servants bound out for five to seven years from the United Kingdom would labor with black servants and might extend their work relationship into sexual liaisons and marriage. Concubinage was a luxury of the wealthy. Porterfield relates accounts about Benjamin Franklin and George Washington engaging in sexual affairs with black women and Alexander Hamilton being mulatto and bearing two black sons. Porterfield also refers to the notorious story of a Thomas Jefferson/Sally Hemings relationship.[1]

---

[1] Readers are referred to the newly published *The Jefferson Scandals: A Rebuttal*. Virginius Dabney presents a convincing argument that Jefferson was the victim of seditious gossip spread by James Callendar, a chronic blackmailer.

The motives for the 1700 and 1800 black-white relationships are discussed. Slave women could be forced to enter sexual relationships with promises and threats and even physical abuse. Slave women might desire relationships because of the closeness to power, the openly apparent competition with white women, and the reciprocal physical attraction. Slave men could display machismo by being with tabooed women and this action could precipitate white mens' aggressiveness, fear, and hostility.

Thirty-three states legislated laws prohibiting interracial marriage. This homogamy and endogamy or the marriage of people from the same group, maintained Puritan morality and slavery. Moreover, it dictated the pool of potential marriage partners, perpetuated the property ownership through family inheritance, and supported the status quo of the social and work worlds.

Porterfield completed a study of current day interracial marriages. Between 1970 and 1974 in Birmingham, Alabama; Cambridge, Ohio; Champaign-Urbana, Illinois; and Jackson, Mississippi he conducted in-depth taped interviews with 40 black-white couples. Thirty-three black male-white female and seven white male-black female couples participated. The couples dated on average 16 months prior to marriage, entered their current marriage at the average age of 24 years, and were married for over five years at the time of the interview. A quarter of the couples were childless; the mean number of children per family was 1.8. After marriage, the couples generally severed their ties with religious and social organizations, becoming "antiorganizational." Both Conner and Porterfield had similar obstacles in obtaining their samples. Porterfield originally contacted 67 couples, 95% of whom had been made known to him by informants. The 27 non-participants were vigorously opposed to involvement in the study and felt that the act of contact had been an invasion of privacy.

Porterfield discusses six theories of black-white mate selection. 1) A pathologically hostile person may marry for control and revenge rather than for love and tenderness. 2) A person may out-marry to display idealistic, non-bigoted liberalism. 3) An individual may be either cosmopolitan or a social misfit and choose friends for personal rather than cultural reasons. Intermarriage could be an act of mutual rejection. 4) An out-marrying person may be rebelling against parental authority and desiring to offend parents on a conscious or unconscious level. 5) An individual may be exhibiting neurotic self-degradation or self-help by marrying interracially. 6) Psychosexual attraction may be the basis for the relationship with a racially different person.

Porterfield concludes that the basis for these six theories of black-white mate selection is on individual cases and small samples and labels these motives "too unsystematic, fragmentary, and often speculative." If love is the primary reason for a marriage, there is no motivational difference between inter and intraracial marriage. In fact, Porterfield as does Conner assert that the act of interracial marriage itself denotes extensive motivation on the part of each spouse.

Porterfield isolates three general categories of motives for mate selection: nonrace-related, race-related, and marginal status of an individual in her or his racial group. Of the 40 couples, 28 black male-white female and three white male-black female couples indicated the motive of love and compatibility. Three black male and white female couples named love and compatibility and added that the white female was less domineering, pregnant, or perceived as a status symbol. Four white male-black female couples stated love and compatibility as motives for selecting their mates and added that the black women involved were admired for their independence and self-sufficiency, were pregnant, or desired to marry a man of comparable education and occupational status. Only two did not indicate love and compatibility and both were black male-white female couples. For one couple, the husband wanted a less domineering white women and to rebel against tradition. His wife was attracted to black men. In the second couple, the husband felt he increased his social status. His spouse perceived herself as an outcast with white people.

Porterfield concludes that the majority of couples in his sample express motives similar to couples who intramarry. Courtship and intimacy can precipitate marriage in spite of differences.

Hawaii–An Intercultural Culture

The Department of Psychiatry of The John A. Burns School of Medicine at the University of Hawaii published a collection of papers titled *Adjustment of Intercultural Marriage*. Hawaii is a polygot of cultural and racial groups. Intermarriage is the norm and not a deviant pattern of behavior as described by Bernard, Conner, and Porterfield. Terence A. Rogers makes this point indicating that over 50% of current marriages in Hawaii are intercultural. Rogers speaks to adjustment problems faced by spouses not reared in an intercultural culture and warns of the problems of childrearing complicated by preconceived assumptions of parents and grandparents.

Danilo E. Ponce contends that advanced means of communication and transportation extend cultures to become more tolerant. Thus, marriages become increasingly individualized.

Walter F. Char stresses that the motivations for intercultural marriages are the same as those for intracultural marriages. Each marriage is based on a complementary combination of conscious and unconscious motives which must be interpreted in regard to the involved cultures, setting, and time.

The following twelve motives suggested by Professor Char are relevant to outgroup marriage. The discerning reader will note that some of these motives pertain to selection of a mate from one's own group or in crossing socio-economic status boundaries.

1. Western marriage values love. Love may be the healthy tie that binds two people as well as the push to be involved in spite of cultural differences.

2. Chance and availability are important motives, especially for intercultural couples.

3. An adventuresome need to be different and an eagerness to be with the new is often a personality trait of partners in an intercultural marriage. This need may be amplified into a narcissistic exhibitionism for attention getting purposes.

4. Reasons may be practical such as improvement of financial and social status.

5. Psychoanalysts believe that one reason for intercultural marriage is the Oedipus/Electra complex. This conflict is experienced by a three to five year old child who has strong positive feelings toward the parent of the opposite sex and competitive and negative feelings toward the parent of the same sex. If these emotions are not resolved one possible outcome can be an exaggerated phobia of incest or the selection of a spouse who is quite different from the opposite sex parent. This can circumvent competition with the same sex parent.

6. Fixation with an early love object may be a motive for a marriage. A person may marry into the culture of an early caretaker.

7. Parental messages expressing satisfaction or lack of satisfaction about marriage may be followed or be the motive for an intercultural marriage based on rebellion.

8. Belief systems about other cultures may be the motive for a marriage. These belief systems may be sexual fantasies which label one group to be more sexual than another. A person uncomfortable with her or his own sexuality my desire the "forbidden fruit" of another culture.

9. A person may feel inferior due to a mental, physical, or social handicap and enter an intercultural marriage after determining that acceptance will be found only outside of the culture of birth. A marriage for this motive may be consciously considered to be a second best or stand-in marriage.

10. Intercultural marriage may be an act of aggression toward another race. Defiance and revenge by one partner can humiliate the in-laws. The partner will generally complement this need by either feeling personally inferior or angry and rebellious against parents, culture, and society.

11. Idealism may be a motive of a "liberal" marrying interculturally. Identification with the underdog, an inferiority complex, rebellion, and rescue could be outgrowths of this idealism.

12. A sadomasochistic intercultural marriage can involve a "slave" who can be controlled, humiliated, hurt, and teased because the partner has alienated family and friends by entering the marriage.

Conclusion

A person marries another person with whom an important level of communication has been reached. The possibilities of open communication and use of available options of communication is severely constrained in most societies. Intermarriage has been controlled by use of closed communities, traditional norms for behavior, matchmakers, language newspapers, bride ads, and correspondence limited to kith and kin.

Yet, the United States has experienced a history of small but significant increase of intermarriage. This has been due in part to the philosophical concept of freedom, a relatively open arms immigration policy since the nation's birth, unplanned migration which limited the number of potential in-group marriage partners available to any cohort in the marriage market and a system of stratification which rewards merit rather than family background and places more importance on class status than ethnic, cultural, or racial background. The rates of intercultural and interracial marriage have been especially advancing with the ever changing communication and transportation technology closing space and providing time to test and experiment with one's interpersonal relationships.

Yet, with all this activity, the literature concerning intercultural and interracial marriage is relatively sparse. The relative dearth of work in this area is a research topic.

In this essay I stress the interplay of geographic, historical, and sociological motives and rationales for intercultural and interracial marriage. Psychological reasons and messages of the media also influence our marital choices be they "Roots" or "As the World Turns." Intermarriages are thought to be progressive endeavors by courageous, idealistic, and strong human beings. This is a view held by optimists. Such unions are unhealthy liaisons entered into by maladjusted neurotics according to pessimists. The psychological dynamics for intermarriage are also found in "straight" marriages. The bottom line is whether the union provides the necessary warmth, love, affection, excitement, caring, intimacy, and solidarity all human beings require. This is the prerequisite behind the masks of two racially different people. "It takes two to tango" and consciously and unconsciously a person selects a marriage partner who complements a particular dance step and road in life.